WORKS BY MRS. SIGOURNEY,

PUBLISHED BY

PARRY & M'MILLAN.

I.

ILLUSTRATED POEMS.

BY MRS. L. H. SIGOURNEY.

WITH THE FOLLOWING ENGRAVINGS ON STEEL FROM DESIGNS BY F. O. C. DARLEY, &c.

PORTRAIT OF THE AUTHOR, engraved by CHENY, from a miniature by FREEMAN.
LANDSCAPE, ... engraved by M. DONGALL.
THE ANCIENT FAMILY CLOCK, . engraved by HUMPHREYS.
THE SCOTTISH WEAVER, . . engraved by HUMPHREYS.
INDIAN SUMMER, . engraved by HUMPHREYS and WILLMORE.
ERIN'S DAUGHTER, . . . engraved by HUMPHREYS.
THE AGED PASTOR, . . . engraved by HUMPHREYS.
THE DIVIDED BURDEN, . engraved by R. HINSHELWOOD.
THE BEAUTIFUL MAID, . . engraved by HUMPHREYS.

This volume is beautifully printed, with large type, on fine white paper, and bound in crimson cloth, extra gilt edges, and in Turkey morocco antique, and super extra.

II.

SELECT POEMS.

BY MRS. L. H. SIGOURNEY.

With Illustrations.

In one handsome 12mo. volume, in cloth binding, and cloth extra gilt edges.

THE

WESTERN HOME,

And Other Poems.

BY

Mrs. L. H. SIGOURNEY.

PHILADELPHIA:
PARRY & M^cMILLAN,
SUCCESSORS TO A. HART, LATE CAREY & HART.
1854.

STEREOTYPED BY L. JOHNSON AND CO.
PHILADELPHIA.

PUBLISHER'S NOTICE.

It may be proper for us to state that this book consists of poems never before published, the longest of which furnishes the title; also of some selections from the illustrated octavo edition of Mrs. Sigourney's Poems, issued from our house, and of a few other poems that have appeared, from time to time, in various periodicals, but have never before been comprised in any volume.

Philadelphia, August, 1854.

CONTENTS.

Mrs. Sigourney's Poems.

THE WESTERN HOME.

HIGH noon, on broad Ohio's tide,—
And while its flashing waters glide,
'Mid fringed bank, or sunny glade,
Or unshorn forest's towering shade,
As erst it flowed ere bold and young
To birth this wondrous century sprung,
In a green thicket dense and rude
Two youths the woodman's toil pursued.
—Their stalwart arms might rule the tide,
Their lips with vermil tinge were dyed,
Brown was the cheek that braved the blast,
  And oft, with clarion swell,
Snatches of merry song were heard
As light through opening vistas peered,
For at their strokes, dealt thick and fast,
  The forest monarchs fell.—

Reclining now on greensward fair,
The simple noontide meal they share,
When one who seemed to muse awhile
Looked up, and said, with kindling smile,
"Sweet is this life, in greenwood here.
  Yet sweeter 'twere, to-day,
If one from our own clime was near,
  Whose name I will not say."

"Speak out! speak out!" his comrade cried,
With flashing red his forehead dyed.
  "I know thou fain wouldst claim
Young Mary Ashton for thy bride:
How vain to seek with bootless shame
From me that truth to hide.
She is the fairest of our band,
The very lily of the land.
  And think'st thou that her sire,
Who frowns if even the zephyr meek
Ruffles the ringlets on her cheek,
  Would yield to thy desire,
And see her in thy footsteps go,
Mid brambly brake and Indian foe?
  Walter St. Clair, I tell thee no."
  Then to his task he sprang,
Nor marked the expression, arch and sly,

That lurked in Walter's eagle eye
  And heard without a pang
Reverberating cliffs prolong
The chorus of his echoed song,
"Oh! Love is sweet, and Love is strong."

And yet, perchance, that manly breast
  Shut in its deepest core
Misgivings more than words confessed;
  For, when the day was o'er,
And long they slept on pallet low
Such sleep as toil alone may know,
Wild dreams unfurled a tragic scene:—
There stood his fair, with gentle mien
And trembling smile and tear-drop sheen,
  As when they parted last,
But the stern father rushed between,
And all their tender purpose banned,
And forced from his, her yielding hand,
  And then, mid thunder-blast,
On a black, storm-tossed flood she lay
By fiend-like creatures row'd away,
While mocking voices from the shore,
Shrieked with hoarse laughter—"*Meet no more!*"
Then stifled moan and frantic start
Betrayed a torture-stricken heart

Till morn arose with sandals gray,
And warned them to the woods away.

The breath of Spring, that Nature hails,
Stole softly o'er New England's vales,
  The lingering snow-wreath fled;
From bough and grove gay carols rang,
And living emerald freshly sprang
  Beneath the elastic tread.
Spring eve amid a garden bower,—
  And though its interlacing vine
Ventured not yet the tender flower
  In flexile wreaths to twine,
Long willow wands their curtain hung,
  And through the leafy screen
That o'er the simple trellis clung,
  A youth and maid were seen.

Of two I spoke, yet three were there,
Though one in vehicle of air
  Eluded mortal eye,
He, whose unfilial arrow keen
Spared not to pierce the Paphian queen,
  That urchin slight and sly.
Around was cast his magic spell,
But what he said I may not tell!

His subtle idiom ill may brook
The cold restraint of pen or book,
  And 'twere a losing part
Here to be painting blush or sigh,
Or whispered vow, or moistened eye,
Which but the pencil of the sky
  Can trace upon the heart.

—Dark night, and 'gainst the window-pane
Dash heavy drops of sleeted rain,
For changeful are New England's skies,
And fickle Spring may violets throw,
Or choke the rills with drifted snow,
  Just as her mood shall rise.
But by a fair, domestic hearth
The large, round logs made crackling mirth,
And musing, as their leaping flame
In every shape fantastic came,
  A man sedate and sage
Was there, the master and the sire:
Time had not quenched his dark eyes' fire
Though threads of silver, here and there,
Lurked mid his wealth of chestnut hair—
The blossomed seed of thought and care
  More than of ripening age.

He mused, perchance, as Priam bent
When his last frustrate shaft was spent,
While a slight form in girlhood's grace
Sate on his knee, her favourite place.
One white arm round his neck was prest,
Her head lay lamblike on his breast,
Yet still within that half-closed eye
Spake woman's deathless constancy.

"Oh, father! since that mother died,
Our dearest solace and our pride,
My aim hath been both day and night
Her place to fill, as best I might;
Yet, ah! how far each highest care
Still fell beneath my hope and prayer,
These bitter tears that nightly flow
And thine oft-tried forbearance show.
—But, father, think! my sister dear,
  Scarce younger is she now,
Than I when in that wo severe
  I saw thy manhood bow,
And clung all trembling to thy side
When the dark grave's brink yawned so wide.
—Put faith in her, she will not fail,
Brave heart may dwell in casket frail:

The willow branch, that breezes sway,
Is firm when oaks are reft away:
And how could I new pleasures share,
If none were left for thee to care?"

"Not for the sadness that must fall,
When thou art gone, on hearth and hall,
Not at the loss it me and mine,
O sweetest daughter! I repine,
For ill befits it one who owes
Mid all his manhood's joys and woes,
To wedded love such countless debt,
Against that love himself to set.
Nor yet to blame thy maiden choice
E'er have I raised the upbraiding voice;
  Mary, if part we must,
Walter, my true friend's noble son,
So well from early boyhood known,
  Is worthy of thy trust.
But I have feared, in western wild,
Lest hardships whelm my cherished child,
Or danger with its iron hail
Should sweep from earth my lily pale.
Alas! in far Ohio's glade
I knew the skulking savage stray'd,

And war-whoop fierce and victim's scream
Too often break my startled dream."

"*God is my strength!*" the maiden said;
And as she gently raised her head,
He marked that steadfast ray
Which o'er her mother's brow did flame
When sudden Death's dark Angel came
To snatch the soul away,
And deemed that pure, prevailing tone
Some echo from her angel throne.
"No longer I resist His will;
Be still, my selfish heart, be still!"

Their stated hour of prayer had gone,
And midnight's step stole slowly on,
Yet on the Book Divine he laid
His reverent hand, and humbly read
The words our blessed Saviour said
To his loved follower, John:—
"Let not your hearts be troubled, ye
Believe in God,—believe in Me."
Then, kneeling side by side,
And hand in hand, the father's prayer
Implored God's pity on their care,

Invoked His aid new toils to bear,
  His grace, whate'er betide.
Methought, that on that hour divine
  The Comforter came down,
He who from earthly griefs can twine
  Heaven's amaranthine crown:
For they, whose eyes so long had wept,
Whose hearts such anxious vigil kept,
Slept their blest sleep who know no guile,
And woke with faith's sustaining smile.

The earliest rose of Summer's care
Now throws fresh fragrance o'er the air,
And o'er full vase and wreathed wall,
Where meekly, mid a festal hall,
Stands one who by her lover's side
Awaits the sacred name of bride.
  And gleaming mid her tresses hung,
Twined with the rose-bud bright and sheen,
A single lily of the vale,
In tender fragrance pure and pale,
By florist's skill beyond its date
Preserved to deck her marriage fête,
Whose emblem flower it long had been
  Amid her playmates young.

There was the priest, of reverend mien,
The thronging friends, the sire serene;
While ranged in beauteous show were seen
Seven graceful heads, a terraced row,
Just as the line of age did go—
  From four to fair eighteen.
Seven steps of life that temple bore,
But at its threshold never more
  The highest shall be seen:
Supply that chasm as best ye may,
Ye, who so long by night and day,
Proud of the elder sister's sway,
  Have counted her your queen.

The rite is o'er, the prayer hath blest,
The bride-ring on the finger prest,
And heartfelt merriment and jest,
  Which the old bridals knew,
Ere fashion's foot had trod them out,
Toss'd their light garlands all about,
  Tinting the cheek with ruddier hue;
Then while the rich collation prest
Its generous warmth on every guest,
The youngest boy, who crept apart
With quivering lip and heaving heart,

Confronted, in a chafing mood,
The manly bridegroom where he stood.
Luther at Augsburg dealt, perchance,
Such fearless and indignant glance.

"Wilt take my sister hence away,
Where bears and Indians tear their prey?"
He stamp'd his foot. "Nay, Walter—nay;
We want her here. We cannot play,
Nor read, nor sing, nor sleep, nor pray—
We can't be good, if she's away."
—Still, as he spoke, his choler rose,
Till mid his hair the crimson glows.
She wrapp'd her white arms round the child,
And soothed and tamed his temper wild;
Yet might you hear amid the bliss
Of her prolonged, protecting kiss,
The sobbing tones, "Go, Walter, go!
You shall not be my brother—no!"

How beautiful is woman's love!
That from the play-place of its birth,
The sister's smile, the parent's hearth,
The earliest warmth of friendship true,
The holy church where first it knew

The balm of Christ's baptismal dew,
To stranger-bands, to stranger-home,
O'er desert clime, o'er ocean foam,
  Goes forth in perfect trust, to prove
The untried toil, the burdening care,
The peril and the pang to dare.
Oh, glorious Love! whose purpose high,
With guardian angel's constancy,
Till severing Death stands sternly by,
Hath to a mortal's keeping given
Its all of earth, its all of heaven.

Heigho! the western hills are steep,
The bridgeless rivers broad and deep;
Nor steam was there, nor iron horse,
With triumph shout and lightning force
  O'er cliff and stream to sweep.
By bridle-path, by blacken'd tree,
Their way they win, if way it be,
  O'er tangled maze and broken sod.
In fragile ark the floods they dare—
Her heart was strong, for *he* was there.
Fast by his side, she felt no fear;
Her more than friend, or brother dear,
  Her more than sire, her next to God.

I've said the road was long and sore,
  Yet no repentant thought was there;
And when the steeds, all travel-wore,
Drew up beside the quiet door
  Of the new home in greenwood fair,
Expect me not in words to say
What joy and deep content had sway
In their fond hearts that happy day.

Their humble roof was firmly laid,
Of jointed logs the building made,
Yet more of space, and comfort too,
Were there than met the careless view;
For well these walls the storm could quell,
And tyrant cold or heat repel.
Nor deem the ingenious Yankee mind,
With woman's household skill combined,
  Fail'd in that home to blend
Somewhat of ornament refined,
  A cheering grace to lend.
Casement, and couch, and table, show
Curtain or cloth like drifted snow,
One precious picture on the walls,
The brow of Mary's sire recalls,
In the bright vase her sister gave,
The sweetest wild-flowers duly wave,

While seeds a brother's care would save
Burst the rich mould and deck the eaves
With clustering buds and lustrous leaves.

And well had Nature done her part
To deck this temple of the heart:
In towering trunks more proud and bold
Than were Dodona's oaks of old,
The beach and sycamore aspire;
And, mid their boughs, with wings of fire
  The red-bird carols clear;
While, hid in interlacing fold,
The parroquets, in green and gold,
  Their crested younglings rear.
Through gleaming vistas, darkly green,
The dun deer's antler'd brow was seen
A moment, ere with graceful bound
He lightly clear'd the enchanted ground,
From rock to rock, in slight cascade,
A silver-footed fountain play'd,
And lavish threw its crystal store
Like diamonds near that sylvan door;
Then dancing on, in freedom wild,
While brightening turf its course confess'd,
To fair Ohio's matron breast
  Leap'd like a joyous child.

How happy is the farmer's toil!
To deck with turf the unsightly soil,
  To clothe the glebe with grain,
Even while he sleeps, the busy seed
Doth wake to consummate his deed,
The earth to bless and man to feed;
  Nor shall his hope be vain,
Who walks with Nature and with God
In holy labor o'er the sod.
And Walter, full of health and zeal,
Went forth each morn such joys to feel.
Nor murmur'd she—that new-made bride—
Though all day long his task he plied;
  For she, with harmonizing will
Her pleasure in her duties found,
  And strove, with still advancing skill,
To make her home's secluded bound
An Eden refuge, sweet and blest,
When, weary, he return'd for rest.

There, too, with matron grace she taught
  The little maiden at her side,
Who in each fitting labour wrought,
  Faithful and satisfied,

For industry with love was blent;
  And well it pleased her gentle guide
To see that docile heart content.
Rain beats the blossoms from the tree,
  Tears wash life's opening joys away—
So let the smile be bright and clear,
And kind the tones that meet the ear
  In childhood's fleeting day.
It comes but once; rob not the year
  Of its sweet spring-tide gay.

Seasons roll'd on; but when again
Blithe summer led her jocund train,
  A new delight it bore.
What was it? Flower of fragrance fair?
Bird of rich song, or plumage rare?
  Fruit of ambrosial store?
No! Fruit nor flower of gorgeous ray,
Nor bird of golden wing might pay
  Her risk and daring brave,
For she had rush'd on death to save
A helpless form, a stranger-prize,
A mystic life that never dies:
Hence on her eye a lustre fell,
  And round her lip a smile was wove,

That, eloquent in silence, tell
  The loss of self in holy love.
Now brought each hour its fair employ,
  While reigned with soft control
That fulness of a woman's joy
  Which ripeneth best the soul,
Which fitteth for the angel's kiss,
In better, purer realms than this—
A mother's lot of care and bliss.

The babe hath learned—(a marvel fraught
  With unsurpassed precocious power!
  For so, within their happy bower,
They, like all other parents, thought)—
  The creeping babe, who almost stands,
Hath learned his father's step to know,
At his young mother's voice to crow,
  And clap his dimpled hands.
But, ah! those secret foes that wait
So thick around life's opening gate,
  Have mark'd that infant fair,
And stolen the laughter from his tongue,
His little, rounded limbs unstrung,
O'er his smooth brow strange pallor flung,
  And woke unslumbering care.

The father sighed each morn to leave
  So anxiously his door,
Yet bade the mother not to grieve,
But with her prayer the hope to weave
  That eve would health restore.

Once, as the day drew near its close,
Affection's piercing wail arose—
"My child! O God! he dies!"
And as the little maiden's eyes,
  Blinded with tears, were raised,
Her shriek burst forth so loud and shrill,
So wild, and ominous of ill,
  The mistress turn'd amazed.
There, in the door, of stature tall,
Bony and gaunt, and sad withal,
She saw a red-brow'd woman stand,
  One of that race
Who, by our people scorned and banned,
Were hunted from their native land,
  Like outcasts base.

Hung on her arm, an ample store,
A scrip replete with herbs she bore,
And drawing near, with aspect wild

Fastened her dark eye on the child,
  And felt his rigid hand,
Then, hasting toward the fire, she shred
  In water pure the leafy gem,
  And groined root, and veined stem,
In which the health-stream slumbered:
She bathed the spasmed limbs and head,
And gently through the shut teeth sped
Reviving drops, and gave with care,
To lungs collapsed, the vital air.

So, though with fear and hatred wild,
  Still cried the little maid aloud,
"Please, do not let her touch the child!"
  Yet, with a spirit bowed,
The mother's yearning heart was still,
Yielding to that strange woman's skill;
  For, as she fanned the flame,
And, kneeling down, the caldron stirred,
A whispered prayer for aid she heard,
  In the Redeemer's name.
And then, as if a mighty spell
On that worn watcher's bosom fell,
She meekly strove, without a moan,
To make God's holy will her own.

So at her side, by night and day,
  Their charge that Indian doctress tended,
Till round his lip those smiles did play,
  Which told their anxious watch was ended;
And then she rose, her way to take,
But fervently the father spake:
"No, stay! Howe'er our God hath made
These differing brows of varying shade,
  His love our hearts hath blent,
And He hath given you grace to bear,
From Death's dread gate our darling fair
  Back, to our soul's content,
So let us make your life our care,
And be our pleasant home your own."

Then answered, in a trembling tone,
She, who to that stern race belonged,
Who, when astonished, pleased, or wronged,
Aim not by outward sign to show
The emotions in their breasts that glow.
"A lodge I have by streamlet lone,
  Far from invading foe;
For my few wants these hands provide,
And better 'tis I there should bide,
  In my poor Indian ways.
But still to you, so free from pride,

This heart its tribute pays;
And if by stern disease you're tried,
I'll stand a sentry at your side,
While through these veins the vital tide
In crimson current strays."

So, when that well-remembered form
Was sometimes seen, at gathering storm
Or nightfall, drawing near,
They hailed her as an honoured guest,
The shelter of their roof-tree prest,
And gave her welcome cheer.
And once, when full of health and glee,
The bantling sate upon her knee,
And mid her dark locks played,
She with their earnest wish complied,
Oft made before, yet oft denied,
The story of her earlier state
Or nation's history to relate,
And simply thus she said:—

"My roving people, well you know,
Subsist by barbed hook and bow;
But of my tribe a favoured few
The arts of agriculture knew—

Reclaimed from savage life, by kind control
  And holiest ministry,
Pupils of one who loved the soul,
  Whate'er the brow might be.
Zeizberger,* blessed saint! how sweet
  His tones at Sabbath-morn,
Would the dear Saviour's words repeat
  From whence our hope was born.
In humble church, where so we joyed to meet,
  Or by our hearth-stones rude,
Methought, his lifted eye of prayer,
His mild, serene, angelic air
Prevailed to win the mercies rare
  That still for us he sued.

With patient hand and tireless thought,
The arts of industry he taught:
Through him the instructed Indian drew
  The sweet blood from the maple tree,
And smiled the laden bough to see
  Where ruddy apples grew.

---

* A village of Christian Indians in Ohio was destroyed, in 1782, by Col. Williamson and his soldiers. It was of the Moravian persuasion, and the grave of its faithful missionary, Zeizberger, is still seen near Zanesville; its inscription stating that he attained the venerable age of 87 years.

The household wheel in music turning round,
The busy loom with jarring sound,
The flying needle's skill,
Wrought out our clothes, while cultured field
Garden and herd, their comforts yield
Obedient to our will.
The rifle that to anguish stirr'd
The flying deer and nestling bird,
Gave place to sickle and to spade,
And harvest-song of youth and maid:
So thus we dwelt, a thriving village fair,
Like children well content to heed a father's care.

"Rumours of war were in the land,
And the pale faces frowned
Whene'er the forest-sons they scanned
Roam o'er their ancient ground;
Yet still Zeizberger's flock was kept
In peace where gentle waters crept
Mid pastures green, from tumult free.
The corn of spring was in its leaf,
The flax-flower waxing blue,
And o'er the fresh buckwheat the bee
A merry reaper flew—

In ripples o'er its rocky bed
The Tuscarawas murmured,
  But not of fear or grief,
For, like a child that's tired of play,
In unsuspicious dreams the quiet hamlet lay.

"But as the lightning cleaves the sky
When summer-suns are warm and high,
  The startled midnight blushed,
  Each cottage roof was red,
From sleep their inmates rush'd,
  And sank among the dead!
White warriors! sure ye found your prey
All unprepared for mortal fray,
With mutter'd curse and flashing sword,
On the slain mother's breast were clinging infants gored,
And e'er the dawning of the day,
  All, all, had ceased to live;
Save two or three, who fled away,—
  Christ help us to forgive!

"Vengeance, the Eternal saith, is mine;
    Yet in the red man's heart,
      Vengeance is strong,
      And liveth long,

Where Christ's love hath no part.
And ambush with its secret line
  Hath bade the white man bleed,
And Crawford * was condemned to make
Atonement at the torture stake,
  For this unrighteous deed.

"My poor old sire, with temples gray,
My husband, in their life-blood lay,
And how I 'scaped, I cannot say,
But for the baby nursling at my breast,
With them I would have gone to rest.
  Life was the harder lot,
Yet ever that reproachful eye
Gazed on me when I wished to die,
  And chained me to the spot.
'I fear thee, babe!' I fain would sigh
  At night, in whispers low,
To the weak thing, too young to know
  What speech did signify,

* Col. William Crawford was taken captive, and burned by the Indians, in Wyandot county, Ohio, in 1782. To his supplication for life, a chief who had formerly been his friend replied, that it might have been granted, but for the recent massacre by the whites under Williamson.

'I fear thee, babe! Stronger than fate thou art,
Stronger than woman's heart,
  Thou wilt not let me die!'
A booth I built, of branches rude,
O'ermastering cliffs the solitude
  Kept secret where we shrank,
God fed us like his raven brood,
  And of the brook we drank.
He was a noble boy and mild,
I fondly watched him as he smiled,
  Yet could not smile on him,
For sounding ever in my ear
Was a great cry of death and fear,
  Like river rushing o'er its brim;
And o'er my brain at midnight hour
Flashed the same flame of fearful power
  That on our village fed,
When of its life, both root and flower
  Were crushed among the dead.
And thus we lived from day to day,
Until God took my child away;
And when I laid him down in clay,
  I wept not o'er that bed so cool and low,
But laugh'd aloud to think he was set free
From man's demoniac tyranny,
  And ne'er their misery could know,

Who, struggling with a mortal wound,
Are in their home's hot ashes drowned.

"Still, close beside that little mound,
  Year after year I dwell;
There doth the earliest blue-bird sing,
There spreads the moth its milk-white wing,
  And, cowering in its leafy cell,
The arbutus sweet is found.
I drive away the screaming owl,
And all unsightly beasts that prowl
  My baby's couch beside.
O friends! your tears are falling fast,
Heaven shield ye from the wrecking blast
  That sweeps life's ocean cold;
God give ye, when its billows moan,
The pity you to me have shown—
  Christ keep ye in his fold!

Yet deem not, though my sky be dark,
  No star benignant cheers;
Though thwarting tides may check the bark,
  It toward its haven steers.
The skill that with our tribes doth dwell,
Each holy plant of health to tell,
Lends solace to my path of wo.

Where hide those precious roots I know,
Where sleep their germs 'neath trackless snow;
And at what starry node or sign
To make them in their vigour mine.
In mine own lodge those stores I lay;
And when it pleaseth God to say
That by their aid the pains that fall
  On his frail children of the clay
I may assuage or heal,
Roused at the blessed call,
No more my loneliness I feel,
No more at sorrow I repine,
  They all have fled away.
"Yea, and I thank Him that his hand
Hath left me desolate and lone;
Like sparrow to the house-top flown
    I spy a better land.
My soul, where earth's last hope is dim,
  And quenched all love and pride,
Springs up, and takes strong hold on Him,
  And will not be denied."

No tear-drop glittered in her eye,
Those burning orbs were red and dry,
And on her bosom bowed her head,
When the sad tale of wo was said.

Years held their course with cloudless mien,
And still the olive branch serene
  Our youthful country bore;
While population, closing round,
Sprinkled with homes the cultured ground,
  On fair Ohio's shore.
And well had Walter's patient hand,
That broke the glebe and tilled the land,
  Been by its fruits repaid,
Nor yet had Mary's prudent care
E'er failed its fitting part to bear;
Hence rose a mansion large and fair,
  As wealth and numbers bade.
There too, in simple guise and free,
Reigned heartfelt hospitality—
  The Genius of the West,
Such as, perchance, in Mamre's tent
Its patriarchal welcome lent;
Though not, alas! too often blest,
In modern times, with angel-guest.

The shelter of his roof to claim,
Once, to St. Clair a stranger came;
Of stature small, yet port of pride,
Symmetrical and dignified;

With martial air and fluent speech,
And manners such as courts might teach,
  And such a piercing eye,
So black, so keen, so deeply set,
I deem, whoe'er that glance had met,
  Lost not its memory.

With legends old, of classic store,
And his own nation's fresher lore,
  He ruled the attentive ear;
Nor spared the gloss of flattery
To the young group that gathered nigh.
What mother's heart that leaps not high
  Her children's praise to hear?
One had a fairy step and air,
Bright sunbeams tinged another's hair,
And violets had expressed their hue
To give the babe its eyes of blue,
That boy in camp or court might rule,
And this surpass his mates at school,
While from one noble brow there shone
The Fabian glance of Washington.

Yet still strange mystery wrapped him round,
  And day by day, as arm in arm

He paced with Walter o'er his ground,
And heedful marked its utmost bound,
He ruled him with a wizard charm.
The plough was in its furrow stayed,
The swains stood idling in the shade,
Their master's will to know;
Much wondering one so prompt to tell
Each hour's allotted business well,
All order should forego.

But Mary soon, with altered air
And cold averted eye,
Accorded the accustomed care
Of hospitality,
While for her husband's weal a prayer
Ascended silently.
I will not say what instinct blest
Had started to her side,
What shield of diamond armed her breast,
And taught with woman's tact to read
A clause within the tempter's creed,
By others undescried.

Once, as she watched alone and late,
Great was her joy to hear

The entering husband close his gate,
  Nor other footstep near.
But his pale brow was marked with care,
As by her side he drew his chair,
  Claiming her private ear
    And tender sympathy.
"Mary St. Clair!—know'st thou that we
  A fiend have harboured here?
A traitor who would burst in twain
The sacred, blood-cemented chain
  That binds our country dear!
Canst thou believe that Aaron Burr,
Conspirator and murderer,
  Hath sunned him in our household smile?
Shrank not his foot the soil to tread,
  His victim's name that bore?*
Did not his heart in secret quake,
As cried that blood, with voice of dread,
  From far Weehawken's shore?
Where fell, beneath his ruthless hand,
The mightiest statesman of our land,
A martyr to his own mistake
  And the assassin's wile.

---

* That part of Ohio was in a county bearing the name of Hamilton.

Fool that I was to lend an ear
  To words of glozing guile;
    My blessed Mary, speak!"
But first her fond lips dried the tear
  That coursed adown his cheek.

"Naught of the treason could I know
That he to you hath deigned to show,
Yet was I oft constrained to see
That false in principle was he,
  Nor bound by God's most holy fear.
Husband! we'll name his name no more,
Save when devotion's flame decays,
And we would wake a warmer praise
  To our Protector, strong and dear,
Who broke the snare, the victory gained,
And left the spirit's wing unstained."

Whoe'er hath stemmed Ohio's flood,
Where infant Marietta stood,
  And gazed, from helm or prow,
  On lavish Nature's show,
Might start to view, on emerald isle,
A lofty, castellated pile,
With tower and turret rising high,
In feudal pride and blazonry;

Or, landing mid the flower-decked sod,
Might deem Calypso's realm he trod,
For Blennerhasset's gold
Had, with magician's wand, upreared
A palace in the wold.

What graceful form on noble steed
Is seen where parting groves recede?
Whose scarlet robes, bedight with gold,
Sweep his gray flank in ample fold;
While, as the fresher zephyrs blow,
Her ostrich plumes float forth like snow?
'Scaped from her hat, her flaxen hair,
Her ivory throat and forehead bare,
Shun not to meet the buxom air,
Some high-born lady sure is she,
For whom the soul of chivalry
Might lift the lance or bend the knee.
So fearlessly she wields the rein,
That, as her courser skims the plain,
She seems of him a part;
Yet not by feats of grace alone
Her best accomplishments are shown;
That higher, holier charm she bears,
By which a wife and mother's cares
Attract and mould the heart.

And Blennerhasset scarce can hide
The promptings of a husband's pride,
  As one so fair and young
Hangs o'er the classic page sublime,
Or pours the speech of many a clime
  Mellifluent from her tongue.

Who sitteth in yon courtly hall,
Where taste refined holds festival,
Admiring, and admired of all?
He of slight form and martial grace,
  And eye so piercing bright,
Its wondrous ray illumes the place
  With strange, unearthly light?
Methinks he seems some hidden snare
To spread with fascinating care,
  Both day and night.

Lord of the Isle! beware! beware!
  A fiend beside thee lurks;
And by thy cold, abstracted air,
Thy scorn of beauty's gentle care,
  I fear the poison works.
To prayer! Hast thou no Friend above
To snatch thee from the snare?

Are fain to linger near his side,
With mournful mien;
Their voice he heeds not, save to chide,
Nor sleeps he, save with sudden start,
And muttered cry of pain or guilt;
Ambition in his noble heart
Hath found a flaw, and, entering, built
A nest for birds unclean.

Oh! summon science to thine aid,
For thou hast loved her well;
And she hath made thy sylvan shade
Her favoured citadel.
Haste! raise thy tube and scan the stars,
Turn History's tome of woes and wars,
Recall Hibernia, seamed with scars,
Thine own dear native isle!
But patriot warmth and classic lore,
Cherished so long, are prized no more;
Pure love, with angel smile,
Melts not ambition's frost—
The spell is clenched, the man is lost.
Alas! he prays not! Deaf to love,
Alone he roams, through bower and grove.
Two cherub boys, so late his pride,

'Twere long to tell, and sore to tread,
Where Burr his hoodwinked victim led,
From risk to risk, from loss to loss,
  A dynasty to found,
Which, like a castle in the air,
When winds and waves their banners toss,
  Sank baseless to the ground.
All burdens still his dupe must bear,
Till, like a bark on breakers tost,
His honour and his wealth were lost.

Conspiracy and treason stored
Grave charges 'gainst the island lord;
Unnumbered ills his steps await,
The felon's bar, the exile's fate—
Dark contrast to his high estate.
And as the doom vindictive falls,
His princely home lies desolate;
Soldiers are quartered in its halls,
And scathing fires deface its walls;
The trampled shrubs and riven flowers
Expire around the rifled bowers,
While, wandering from his loved domain,
  He turns to realms beyond the sea,
Appealing for redress in vain
  From his betrayer's perfidy.

Still, that true wife is by his side,
Not o'er lost Paradise to sigh,
But share his lot, whate'er betide,
With woman's deathless constancy.

Yet who shall lift with pity pale,
From future years the incumbent veil?
Yon widowed form,—to penury left,
Of every earthly hope bereft,
Who sinks unaided mid the strife,—
Can that be Blennerhasset's wife?
—At her low grave by stranger hands
Obscurely made, one mourner stands,
A man* oppress'd by want and care,
A prey to sickness and despair,
Can that be Blennerhasset's heir?
—Alas! that bitter streams should spread
So wide, from one dark fountain-head.

Oh Aaron Burr!—with talents proud
To dazzle or control the crowd,
Whose dauntless courage never quailed,
Though dangers frowned, or foes prevailed,

* Herman Blennerhasset, the last remnant of an unfortunate and once happy family, is said still to reside in New York, the victim of disease and poverty.

I saw thee, when thy sun drew low,
And fourscore winters dimmed thy brow,
And state and wealth and friends had fled,
And all of kindred blood were dead,
Yet flashed that eye, unquenched and bright,
Forth from the loneliness of night
And frost of age.—Say, was its light
What heaven on its own planets turneth?—
Or from the pit that ever burneth?—
—But thou art gone, nor would we tread
  Thine ashes with too stern a blame,
For thou dost teach us from the dead
  A lesson that all pride should tame;
That genius high and morals base
  Mar the great Giver's plan,
And, like a comet's flaming race,
Make visible the deep disgrace
  Of His best gifts to man.

Still in those cares, remote from strife
That marked the happy farmer's life
  Walter St. Clair and Mary dwelt,
And still their genial influence felt.
High health was theirs and cheerful thought,
Sweet sleep that knows nor spasm nor cry
Of undigested luxury,

Fond Love, unswerving and unbought,
For which in vain the heart must sigh
That, moved by calculation cold,
Its holiest vows hath bartering sold
For fashion, or for thirst of gold.
The venal hand may diamonds link,
In velvet piled the foot may sink,
The lips from jewelled chalice drink,
Yet every nerve to joy be dead,
And all the life of feeling fled
In the heart's palsied atrophy.

Like the unfoldings of a dream
In transmutation strange,
A swollen, unquelled, unebbing stream,
Swept on the tide of change:
For where, of old, from copse and brake
The lonely owl discordant spake,
Or wolf and panther sprang,
Where round the settler's cabin low
The prowling Indian bent his bow
Or savage war-whoop rang,
The warehouse peers, the merchants throng,
The costly chariot rolls along,
Tall spires like guardian angels bless,
O'erflowing schools their lore impress,

While through the streets, in ceaseless tide,
A hundred thousand people glide.
Walter and Mary, side by side
  The magic drama viewed,
Filled with a patriot's glòwing pride,
  A Christian's gratitude;
And e'er their sun of life went down
  To its unclouded rest,
Had Cincinnati won her crown
  Queen of the West.

And they had aided, heart and hand
The weal of that adopted land,
  Each in their own blest way,
Of order, he, and honest trust
And manly virtues, pure and just,
  Foundation firm to lay,—
And she, in woman's quiet sphere,
The plants of household good to rear,
And light on ignorance to shed.
Nor other rights she coveted
  Than to such sphere belong.
Perchance, at first, with critic eye
Her course was scanned suspiciously,
  Yet still in meekness strong

She shared with want her daily bread,
Like angel watched the sufferer's bed
Till in her steps the grateful trod,
And praise for her went up to God.

As strikes its root 'neath tropic sky
The blessed banian's canopy,
Nor rests until its stems have made
Deep continuity of shade,
And its impervious foliage wove
For man a bower, for birds a grove,
So stretched their life in truth and grace,
A blessing to their numerous race,
While its sweet seeds without a thorn
Sprang up to blossom for the unborn.

But when his active years had fled,
  And those of rest drew nigh,
Such form erect, elastic tread,
  And clear, observant eye,
St. Clair retained, that those who met
The pressure of his friendly hand,
  And smile of welcome cheer,
  Heard with a skeptic ear
That full fourscore their seal had set
  Upon his features bland.

Dewed was his grave with many a tear
That mourned the honored pioneer,
Who with a chain of bright good will had clasped his
young country dear.
Oh! let such links be multiplied,
And with their heart-wove net-work wide
Bind north to south, and east to west:—
Nor aught thy unity molest,
My Land! around whose cradle-bed
The glorious fathers prayed and bled,
And mingled with their battle-cry
The watch-word,—God and Liberty.—

Awhile beyond her life's best friend
Did Mary's pilgrimage extend,
Darkened, but not dismayed;
For on an Arm divinely strong
Leaning in faith, she passed along
The solitary shade;
And beautiful it was to see
What tender, filial ministry
Her faithful cares repaid.
There are, who deem that age must be
Ever unlovely to the sight,
That when the locks grow thin and white
No charm can light the face,

Yet every season hath its grace
To the meek eye that skills to trace
   And read God's works aright.

Young children clustering round her chair,
Her wealth of storied lore to share,
Believed that beauty still was there;
And youth who lingered at her side,
Seeking her wisdom for their guide,
   Beheld, with reverent air,
That holy smile of calm content,
The twilight of a life well spent,—
Kindness no differing creed could bound,
Warm sympathy for all around,—
While still her beaming eye confest
The joy of making others blest.
   So, when in hope serene
   She changed this earthly scene
   Love's tear upon her pillow lay,
And hallowed memories from the burial clay
   Sprang up in fadeless green.

MEMORY.

THE past she ruleth. At her touch
  Its temple valves unfold,
And from their gorgeous shrines descend
  The mighty men of old.
At her deep voice the dead reply,
  Dry bones are clothed and live,
Long-perished garlands bloom anew,
  And buried joys revive.

When o'er the *future* many a shade
  Of saddening twilight steals,
Or the dimmed *present* to the soul
  Its emptiness reveals,
She opes her casket, and a cloud
  Of cheering perfume streams,
Till with a lifted heart we tread
  The pleasant land of dreams.

Make friends of potent Memory,
O young man, in thy prime;
And with her jewels bright and rare,
Enrich the hoard of Time,
For, if thou mockest her with weeds,
A trifler mid her bowers,
She'll send a poison through thy veins,
In life's disastrous hours.

Make friends of potent Memory,
O maiden, in thy bloom;
And bind her to thine inmost heart,
Before the days of gloom,
For sorrow softeneth into joy
Beneath her wand sublime,
And she immortal robes can weave ·
From the frail threads of Time.

THE MOHAWK WARRIOR.

STRETCHED on his bed of skins, the Panther lay,
The warrior of the Mohawks. Low and dark
Was his lone cabin, near the brawling stream,
While o'er its walls the hunter's shaggy spoils
Profusely hung. In the stone chimney rude,
The flame went crackling up.
But there he lay,
That gray-haired chieftain, to arise no more.
His son, the sole companion of the lodge,
Was by his side. Immovable he stood,
Like a tall bronzed statue, sculptured bold,
In massive strength.
Symmetrical was he,
That warlike sire, whose frame had scorned to bend
'Neath ninety winters, and whose deep-set eye
Flashed in its struggle with an unseen foe,
Plucking his heart-strings.

Painfully he spake:
"Son of the Fawn! the Panther leaps no more;
His teeth no more are terrible. Time was"—
On his chill lip the laboured accents died.
Still o'er him swept the *past*, the battle-cry,
The forest-hunt, the midnight council-fire.
"*Time was*"—

In vain he strove, a smothered groan
O'ercame his utterance. Yet the anguish passed,
And he, whose strength had never quailed before,
Exhausted, slumbered like a helpless child.

He woke, and by him stood that statued son,
Watching the spoiler's progress o'er his brow,
With a red, restless eye.

"*Air! air!*" he cried,
With a wild gasp. Upon its utmost hinge
The rough door swung. The lungs, collapsing, caught
That blessed draught, and light to heart and eye
Spontaneous sprang.

Once more the sufferer marked
The brook contending with the fitful winds,
While the full autumn-moon, through parted boughs,
Silvered the flashing waters, as they plunged
O'er a steep ledge.

On the fair sight he fed,

With wistful glance, as one who takes his leave,
Ne'er to return. His long and toil-worn life
Seemed as a span, while a sharp lance's point
Traced hurrying scenes on memory's shrivelled scroll.

"I sing no death song. War, that once I loved,
Fades in its own foul smoke. But, *she* is there—
There, by that stream's green edge. Just so the moon
Looked down upon us, when she first was mine.
Child of the Fawn! her eye was like its beam
On yonder troubled waters. When I came
Wearied from hunting, or the strife of men,
Such was it in my soul.
                                        She waits me still—
She, whom alone I loved. She waits me there,
In yon bright forests, where our unquelled sires
Roam as of old.
                                        I'll tell her in her ear,
That thou dost linger, by the river's brink
So, to this cabin we'll together come,
And talk with thee."
                                        Breath failed him, for he spake
Rapid and fervent. He who ne'er had known
A dear Redeemer's dying love, or heard
The angel's song, "peace and good-will to men,"
Turned to the *one lone day-star* of his course,

And the pure passion of his heart's first love
Shed light on death's grim face.
"I made her grave
By the great western lake. Deep, deep and dark!
The mound is high above it. The blue waves
Break round its feet. Thy mother slumbers there.
I'll go and see that grave before I die."

Half from his bed he sprang. The giant limbs
Which like the oak that braves a century's wrath,
Had never failed, grew rigid.
Back he fell,
Dashing the water from the hand that fain
His parching lips would lave, and with glazed eyes
Gibbered and murmured, as delirium claimed
Tyrannic service from a stiffening tongue.
Then, mid a labyrinth of sighs and smiles,
And moans, and snatches of unuttered words,
And shivering spasms, to which the worn-out nerves
Scarce gave sensation, or response of pain,
Death came and did his work, and the dark clay
Lay still, before him.
And that lonely lodge
Of the fierce Panther of the Mohawks, heard
Naught save the loud lamenting of his son;
For pride no longer checked the filial flood,

Wnen none were near to say, "*Our chieftain weeps.*"
So there he stood, an emblem of his race
Whose glory had departed. There he drooped,
And moaned, till dawn had sped on pinions gray,
And day came freshly forth.
But then he strode,
With steadfast step, and eye that told no tale
Of the heart's secret grief, and spake unmoved
The summons to his tribe, who mournful came
Flocking with heads declined, to lay the bones
Of their old warrior in an honoured tomb.

THE SPRING CONCERT.

COME, come to the concert of gladness and glee,
The programme is rich, and the tickets are free.
In a grand vaulted hall, where's there's room, and to
spare,
With no gas-lights to eat up the oxygen there.
The musicians are skilled in their wonderful art,
They have compass of voice, and the gamut by heart,
They travelled abroad in the winter recess,
And sang to great crowds with unbounded success,
And now 'tis a favour and privilege rare
Their arrival to hail, and their melodies share:

These exquisite minstrels a fashion have set,
Which they hope you'll comply with, and will not regret—
They don't keep late hours, for they've always been told
'Twould injure their voices, and make them look old;
But invite you to come, if you have a fine ear,
To the garden or grove, their rehearsals to hear.

Their chorus is full ere the sunbeam is born,
Their music is sweetest at breaking of morn;
'Twas learned at Heaven's gate, with its rapturous lays,
And may teach you, perchance, its own spirit of praise.

THE SPIRIT OF BEAUTY.

Spirit of beauty,—who dost love to dwell
In the pure chalice of yon new-born flower,
That unrepining shares my wintry cell,
And from my hand receives the mimic shower;

Spirit,—who hoverest o'er the babe's repose,
Where guardian angels bend with viewless kiss,
Counting the innocence no guile that knows
A faint reflection of their higher bliss;

Spirit,—who on the humblest lip doth rest,
That uttereth words of kindness,—and art seen
In the calm sunshine of the lowly breast,
Garnering its treasure in a clime serene;

Spirit,—who, mid the smile of holy age,
Closing its course in hope, dost make abode,
Though Time hath ploughed the brow with tyrant rage,
And scattered snows where sunny tresses flowed;

Sweet Spirit, trembling through the loneliest star
  That the storm-driven mariner descries,
And from the rush-light, when its beam afar
  Eye of his cot—the way-worn peasant spies:

Blest Spirit, touch our hearts, and as the child,
  Who toward his parents' home doth singing hie,
Espies some wanderer, shivering on the wild,
  And leads him onward with a pitying eye,

So, point us to our Father!—He who bade
  Thee in this wilderness his way prepare,
And by thy pure, refining influence aid
  Upward to Him,—First perfect and First fair.

GETHSEMANE.

There was a garden near Jerusalem,
Where Jesus went to pray; not the fair breast
Of Olivet, beloved by Kidron's wave,
But wrapped in denser shades, and deeper veiled,
For the soul's secrecy.
                                        Thither he went,
With his disciples, when his course on earth
Drew near a close. It was a moonless night,
And heavily he drooped, as one who bears
An inward burden. Drear Gethsemane
Gave him no welcome, when his weary feet
Paused at its portal. Almost it might seem
That Nature, with prophetic eye, foresaw
The sufferings of her Lord. With its rough cones,
The terebinth did tremble, and the buds
That Spring had early wakened, hid their heads
Again in their turf cradles, tearfully.

A horror of great darkness fell on Him
Who wrought the world's salvation.
Unto those,
Who at His call had left the fisher's coat,
And the receipt of custom, and had shared
His daily bread, He turned; for in the hour
Of bitter anguish, sympathy is dear,
Even from the humblest.
Unto them He turned,
But they were gone,—*gone!* and He searching found
That heavy-eyed and self-indulgent band
Stretched out, in sleep supine. They took their rest,
While He, who for their sakes had toiled and taught,
And healed their sickness and supplied their need,
And walked at midnight on the raging sea,
Strove with the powers of darkness. Rising tides
Of grieved, untiring, unrequited Love
Mixed with the question from those lips divine,
"*Could ye not watch one hour?*"
Then, He withdrew
Again, and prayed. The mournful olives bent,
Weaving their branches round him tenderly,
And sighed and thrilled, through all their listening leaves.
Paler than marble was the brow that pressed

The matted grass, leaving the blood-print there,
Yea, the red blood-print.
Oh, Gethsemane!
Draw closer thy dark veil. I would not see
My Saviour's agony.
Yet not alone
Passed that dread hour, though His disciples slept,
There was a pitying spirit of the skies
Who wept and wondered, and from odorous wings
Shed balm ambrosial on the sufferer's head.

Would that I knew *his* name, who thus did stand
Near our Redeemer, when both earth and heaven
Forsook his fainting soul. There was a sound
Like rushing pinions of a seraph host;
But wildering awe and unsolved mystery
Enchained them in mid-air, and only one
Came down to comfort Him.
Thou who didst bear
Unuttered pangs for an ungrateful race,
Remember us, when desolate, and lone,
In our Gethsemanes, we agonize,
Imploring God to take the cup away,
And shrinking, in our poverty of faith,
To add the words, that make His will, our own.

Thou, who amid Heaven's bliss, forgettest not
The weakness of the clay Thou once didst wear,
Nor how the shafts of pain do trouble it,
Send us a strengthening angel, in our need,—
Oh! be Thyself that angel.

WILD FLOWERS.

FLOWERS of God's planting!—Man doth call ye *wild*,
Though in your breasts a gentle nature lies,
And timidly ye meet the breezes mild,
Paying their love-kiss with your perfumed sighs.
Still, with unuttered speech,
More true philosophy ye teach,
Than they, your rich-robed relatives, who share
The florist's tender care,
And shrink with fretted nerves from the too buxom air.

Methinks their polished petals hide
Some thrill of vanity or pride,
As the admiring throng
Through the rich green-house press along,
Where still they claim, in proud magnificence,
A warmer smile than Heaven's own healthful skies
dispense,

Or lulled on beauty's breast
To a brief dream of rapturous rest,
Too soon—with pale, regretful eye
Fulfil their envied destiny, and die.

But ye, in humble cell,
Cloven nook or grassy dell,
Or by the brooklet's shaded brim,
Turn in your trustful innocence to Him,
Who wisely metes the sun-beam and the rain;
Or else the plough-share's fatal pain,
Or even the crushing foot repay
With a forgiving fragrance—and beneath
The same loved skies that gave you birth,
On prairie broad, or purple heath,
Pass willingly away
From your slight hold on earth.

Perchance, with longer date
Gladdening the field-bee, at her work elate,
Ye nurse your buds, and give your winged seeds
Unto the winnowing winds, to sow them as they fly
In fertile soil, or mid the choking weeds
Or desert sands, where the rank serpent feeds;
Then, not of death afraid,
All unreluctantly ye fade,

Meek as ye bloomed at first, in glen, or forest-glade,
Bequeathing a sweet memory
Unto the scented turf, where erst ye grew,
And garnered in your souls the heaven-distilling dew.

Oh, fair, uncultured flowers!
The charm of childhood's roving hours,
Who seek no praise of man—have ye not caught
The spirit of ***His*** lowly thought,
Who loved the frail field-lily—and the bird
By whom its breast was stirred?
And on his mountain-shrine
With eloquence divine
From its unfolded leaves, as from a text book, taught?
Yes—still ye show, in lessons undefiled,
The Christian life and death, though man doth call ye *wild.*

DEATH OF CARDINAL MAZARIN.

Two months, the questioned healer said,
And turned him from the place,
While every tint of colour fled
That dark Italian face,—
Heart-struck was he, whom France obeyed,
Peasant, and prince, and peer,
And with the clank of fetters made
Rich music for his ear.

Proud Ann of Austria lowest bent
With subjugated soul,
And Ludovicus Magnus scarce
Withstood his stern control,
While distant nations feared the man
Who ruled in court and bower;
Yet those slight words dissolved the spell
Of all his pomp and power.

Before him passed his portioned line,
  Mancini's haughty race,
Jewels and coronets they wore,
  With cold and thankless grace;
And for a payment poor as this,
  Had he his conscience grieved?
And marred with perjured hand the cross
  His priestly vow received?

Beside him strode a spectral form,
  Still whispering in his ear,
"*Make restitution!*" fearful sound,
  That none besides might hear;
"*Make restitution!*" But the spoil
  From earth and ocean wrung,
By countless chains and wreathed bands,
  Around his spirit clung.

"*Two months! two months!*" these frightful words
  Could all his peace destroy,
And poison the enamelled cup
  Where sparkled every joy,
They met him in the courtly hall,
  They silenced song and tale,
Like those dead fingers on the wall
  That turned Belshazzar pale.

Once in his velvet chair he dreamed,
But rocking to and fro,
His restless form and heaving breast
Betrayed a rankling wo:
"*Two months! two months!*" he murmured deep,
Those fatal words were there,
To grave upon his broken sleep
The image of despair.

Uncounted wealth his coffers told,
From rifled king and clime,
His flashing gems might empires buy,
But not an hour of time,
No! not a moment. Inch by inch,
Where'er he bent his way,
That grim pursuer steadfast gained
Upon the shrinking prey.

His pulseless hand a casket clutched,
Though Death was near his side,
And 'neath the pillow lurked a scroll
He might no longer hide;
While buried heaps of hoarded gain
In rust and darkness laid,
Bore witness to the Omniscient Eye
Like an accusing shade.

But on the King of Terrors came
  With strong, relentless hold,
And shook the shuddering miser loose
  From all his idol gold,
And poorer than the peasant hind
  That humbly ploughs the sod,
Went forth that disembodied mind
  To stand before its God.

FALLEN FORESTS.

Man's warfare on the trees is terrible.
He lifts his rude hut in the wilderness,
And, lo! the loftiest trunks, that age on age
Were nurtured to nobility, and bore
Their summer coronets so gloriously,
Fall with a thunder sound to rise no more.
He toucheth flame unto them, and they lie
A blackened wreck, their tracery and wealth
Of sky-fed emerald, madly spent, to feed
An arch of brilliance for a single night,
And scaring thence the wild deer, and the fox,
And the lithe squirrel from the nut-strewn home,
So long enjoyed.
He lifts his puny arm,
And every echo of the axe doth hew
The iron heart of centuries away.
He entereth boldly to the solemn groves
On whose green altar tops, since time was young

The wingéd birds have poured their incense stream
Of praise and love, within whose mighty nave
The wearied cattle from a thousand hills
Have found their shelter mid the heat of day;
Perchance in their mute worship pleasing Him
Who careth for the meanest He hath made.
I said, he entereth to the sacred groves
Where nature in her beauty bows to God,
And, lo! their temple arch is desecrate.
Sinks the sweet hymn, the ancient ritual fades,
And uptorn roots and prostrate columns mark
The invader's footsteps.

Silent years roll on,
His babes are men. His ant-heap dwelling grows
Too narrow—for his hand hath gotten wealth.
He builds a stately mansion, but it stands
Unblessed by trees. He smote them recklessly
When their green arms were round him, as a guard
Of tutelary deities, and feels
Their maledictions, now the burning noon
Maketh his spirit faint. With anxious care,
He casteth acorns in the earth, and woos
Sunbeam and rain; he planteth the young shoot,
And props it from the storm; but neither he,
Nor yet his children's children, shall behold
What he hath swept away.

Methinks, 'twere well
Not as a spoiler or a thief to prey
On Nature's bosom, that sweet, gentle nurse
Who loveth us, and spreads a sheltering couch
When our brief task is o'er. O'er that green mound
Affection's hand may set the willow tree,
Or train the cypress, and let none profane
Her pious care.
Oh, Father! grant us grace
In all life's toils, so, with a steadfast hand
Evil and good to poise, as not to pave
Our way with wrecks, nor leave our blackened name
A beacon to the way-worn mariner.

8

VIRGINIA DARE.

[The first-born child of English parents in the Western World was the granddaughter of Governor White, who planted a short-lived colony at Roanoke, Virginia, in the year 1587.]

'TWAS lovely in the deep greenwood
  Of old Virginia's glade,
Ere the sharp axe amid its boughs
  A fearful chasm had made;
Long spikes of rich catalpa flowers
  Hung pendent from the tree,
And the magnolia's ample cup
  O'erflowed with fragrance free:

And through the shades the antlered deer
  Like fairy visions flew,
And mighty vines from tree to tree
  Their wealth of clusters threw,
While winged odours from the hills
  Reviving welcome bore,
To greet the stranger bands that came
  From Albion's distant shore.

Up rose their roofs in copse and dell,
  Outpealed the labourer's horn,
And graceful through the broken mould
  Peered forth their tasseled corn,
While from one rose-encircled bower,
  Hid in the nested grove,
Came, blending with the robin's lay,
  The lullaby of love.

There sang a mother to her babe—
  A mother young and fair—
"No flower like thee adorns the vale,
  O sweet Virginia Dare!
Thou art the lily of our love,
  The forest's sylph-like queen,
The first-born bud from Saxon stem
  That this New World hath seen!

"Thy father's axe in thicket rings,
  To fell the kingly tree;
Thy grandsire sails o'er ocean-brine—
  A gallant man is he!
And when once more, from England's realm,
  He comes with bounty rare,
A thousand gifts to thee he'll bring,
  Mine own Virginia Dare!"

As sweet that mother's loving tones
  Their warbled music shed,
As though in proud baronial hall,
  O'er silken cradle-bed,
No more the pomps and gauds of life
  Maintained their strong control,
For holy love's new gift had shed
  Fresh greenness o'er her soul.

And when the husband from his toil
  Returned at closing day,
How dear to him the lowly home
  Where all his treasures lay.
"O, Ellinor! 'tis naught to me,
  The hardship or the storm,
While thus thy blessed smile I see,
  And clasp our infant's form."

No secret sigh o'er pleasures lost
  Convulsed their tranquil breast,
For where the pure affections dwell
  The heart hath perfect rest.
So fled the Summer's balmy prime,
  The Autumn's golden wing,
And Winter laid his hoary head
  Upon the lap of Spring.

Yet oft, with wily, wary step,
  The red-browed Indian crept
Close round his pale-faced neighbour's home,
  And listened while they slept;
But fierce Wingina, lofty chief,
  Aloof, their movements eyed,
Nor courteous bowed his plumed head,
  Nor checked his haughty stride.

John White leaped from his vessel's prow,
  He had braved the boisterous sea,
And boldly rode the mountain-wave—
  A stalwart man was he.
John White leaped from his vessel's prow,
  And joy was in his eye;
For his daughter's smile had lured him on
  Amid the stormiest sky.

Where were the roofs that flecked the green?
  The smoke-wreaths curling high?
He calls—he shouts—the cherished names,
  But Echo makes reply.
"Where art thou, Ellinor! my child!
  And sweet Virginia Dare!
O, silver cloud, that cleaves the blue
  Like angel's wing—*say where!*

"Where is the glorious Saxon vine
  We set so strong and fair?"
The stern gray rocks in mockery smiled,
  And coldly answered, "*where!*"
"Ho! flitting savage! stay thy step,
  And tell—" but light as air
He vanished, and the falling stream
  Responsive murmured—"*where!*"

So, o'er the ruined palisade,
  The blackened threshold-stone,
The funeral of colonial hope,
  That old man wept—alone!
And mournful rose his wild lament,
  In accents of despair,
For the lost daughter of his love,
  And young Virginia Dare.

MICAH AND THE LEVITE.

Judges, 17th and 18th Chapters.

"MOTHER! the hoarded silver, at whose loss
Thou cursedest bitterly, behold! 'tis here!—
I took it."
Thus unhumbled Micah spake—
Nor she reproved, but blessed him, and well pleased
With her recovered pelf, exulting cried,
"The treasure all was dedicate, my son,
Unto a sacred purpose. I had vowed
To make a graven and a molten god,
That we might have our household deities
Always beside us."
So, she counted out
The shekels in his hand, and he, unmoved
At her idolatry, with impious zeal
An ephod and a teraphim prepared.
And then, a wandering Levite—strange to say—
For hireling gain, consented to conduct
The mingled rites, to image, and to God,
Idolatrous and vain. For in those days

There was no king in Israel. Every man
Lived as he listed, doing what was right
In his own eyes.
Forth from the tribe of Dan,
A lawless multitude, intent on spoil,
Marauding o'er the country, in a glen
Of cedar-wrapped Mount Ephraim, found the abode
Of Micah, and upon his cherished gods
Laid sacrilegious hands.
"What dost thou here,
Thou son of Levi?" arrogantly asked
The renegado leader.
"Here I dwell,
Even as a priest, and father to mine host—
Cared for, and paid by him, and well content
To worship at his altar."
"Hold thy peace—
Lay hand upon thy mouth, and come with us—
For whether it is better thus to serve
A solitary house, or be the priest
O'er a whole tribe of Israel, thou canst judge
As well as we."
With dull and earth-bowed eye
The plodding man considered. On one side
Were his ten yearly shekels, robes, and bread
At Micah's table. On the other seemed

Naught save a roaming life, 'mid warrior horde—
Perhaps no sacrificial lamb—not even
A mess of pottage, rich with lentiles brown,
Savory and well beloved. His stupid brow
Long wrought with struggles of unwonted thought,
And longer still had wrought, by doubt perplexed,
Had not ambition, which may find a place
Even with ignoble natures, thrown its bait,
Secret and sure—*the priesthood of a tribe—*
And tithe of victor-spoils.

Quick, upward flew
In lightened scale, the fireside and the board,
All grateful memories—all uttered vows,
That bound him to his patrons and their shrine.
So with the stolen goods he went his way,
Unquestioned still by conscience, if, indeed,
Such monitor he had. In swift pursuit,
With gathered neighbors, sudden roused to arms,
Indignant Micah came. To his sharp words,
Upbraiding bitterly, the Danite chief
Laconic spake, as sworded men are wont,
Who have the power:

"Let not thy voice be heard
Among us here, lest angry fellows rush
On thee, and on thy kindred, and the end
Be worse than the beginning."

With a curse
Of vengeful hatred on the recreant priest,
Who, shrinking in the centre of the host,
Scarce raised a cowering glance, chafed Micah turned
Back to his mother, the contempt and loss
Bearing, as best he might.

Such were the times
In Israel, when each man did what seemed right
In his own eyes. Ill fares it with a land
Where lust of gold, and wayward passions fill
The place of righteous law.

May our own realm,
By Heaven's blest page instructed, give its aid
To order, and authority, and peace,
And heartfelt worship of the God from whom
All blessings flow.

NATURE'S TRUE FRIENDS.

THE insect tribes go wandering by,
Each for himself, the bee's keen eye
Scans where the honied nectaries lie ;
The butterfly coquetteth free
With zephyr, sunbeam, shrub and tree,
The banker Ant, his gains doth hoard,
With forethought, for his winter board,
The plodding beetle onward wends,
The locust hath his private ends,
And rears the warlike wasp with care
His architecture rude and rare.

So, with the birds, careering high,
Some straw to build their nest they spy,
Nor spare to steal the tissues fine
With tapestry its couch to line.
Then close in secret nook they bide,
Their dearest joys from us to hide,

Or soaring, taunt our earth-born care
With happiness we may not share,
Save that we gather from the air
Snatches of melody, that tell
Of higher climes, where angels dwell,
Or echoes of their heaven-taught lay
To warn us of a brighter day.

But ye, meek flowers, with love so true,
Unselfish, constant, ever new,
For us alone, from prisoning dust,
To beauty and to bloom ye burst,
To us ye give, on hill and plain
Your all, requiring nought again;
With lavish trust, your noblest powers,
Blush, odour, solace, life, are ours,
Reserving nought, save one sweet sigh
That breathes at last, that lesson high
How innocence and peace can die.

QUEEN PHILIPPA.

EDWARD was fired with rage.—
"Bring forth," he said,
"The hostages, and let their death instruct
This contumacious city."
Forth they came—
The rope about their necks—those patriot men,
Who nobly chose an ignominious doom
To save their country's blood. Famine and toil,
And the long siege, had worn them to the bone,
Yet from their eye spoke that heroic soul
Which scorns the body's ill. Father and son
Stood side by side, and youthful forms were there,
By kindred linked—for whom the sky of life
Was bright with love—yet no repining sigh
Darkened their hour of fate. Well had they taxed
The midnight thought, and nerved the wearied arm,
While months and seasons thinn'd their wasted ranks.

The harvest failed—the joy of vintage ceased,
Vine-dresser and grape-treader manned the walls;
And when they sank with hunger, others came,
Of cheek more pale, perchance, but strong at heart.
Yet still those spectres poured their arrow-flight,
Or hurled the deadly stone, while at the gates,
The Conqueror of Cressy sued in vain.
"Lead them to die!" he bade.

In noble hearts
There was a throb of pity for the foe
So fallen, and so unblenching; yet none dared
Meet that fierce temper with the word, *forgive!*

Who comes with hasty step, and flowing robe,
And hair so slightly bound? *The Queen! The Queen*
An earnest pity on her lifted brow,
Tears in her azure eye like drops of light,
What seeks she, with such fervid eloquence?—
Life for the lost! and ever as she fears
Her suit in vain, more wildly heaves her breast,
In secrecy of prayer, to save her lord
From cruelty so dire, and from the pangs
Of late remorse. At first, the strong resolve
Curled on his lip, and raised his haughty head,
While every firm-set muscle, prouder swelled
To iron rigour. Then, his flashing eye

Rested upon her, till its softened glance
Confessed contagion from her tenderness,
As with a manly and chivalrous grace
The boon he gave.—
Oh, Woman!—ever seek
A victory like this; with heavenly warmth
Still melt the icy purpose, and preserve
From error's path the heart that thou dost fold
Close in thine own pure love. Yes, ever be
The advocate of sorrow, and the friend
Of those whom all forsake: so may *thy* prayer
In thine adversity, be heard of Him
Who loveth to show mercy.

THE DESTROYER.

There is a ceaseless shaft that speeds
Unerring through the air,
A sleepless archer all unseen,
Yet active everywhere.

Close on tne steps of busy life
He like a shadow glides,
Mysterious checks the bosom's strife,
And chills its purple tides.

The strongly armed and watchful guard,
Who keep the palace gate,
Saw not the entering foe that smote
Their monarch in his state.

The lonely cot's unlifted latch
No roaming robber fears,
Yet there he lurks,—beneath the thatch,—
Ye know it—by the tears.

And though he loves a lofty mark,
The great, the good, the fair,
Still, mid the humblest things that breathe,
Look!—for you'll find him there.

The deer, that feels the hunter's sting,
And struggles on the plain,—
The bird, that fain with broken wing
Would reach its nest again,—

The moth, that flutters round the flower,—
The worm, within that coils,—
He scorneth not his bow to bend,
And glean these lowly spoils.

The mountain strives beneath the cloud
Its hoary head to hide,
The combing billows fain would shroud
The sea's unfathomed pride,—

It may not be,—the hardiest pin
That clothes the Alpine steep,
The mightiest monsters of the brine
That lash the foaming deep,

Confess his power,—the wounded whale
  With crimson stains the tide,
The radiant dolphin waxeth pale,
  As though a rainbow died,—

The sea-horse on the whelming surge
  Floats by, without a moan,
The coral insect builds its tomb,
  And hardens into stone.

He scans the forest, dark with years,
  The palm, the banyan's shade,
The iron oak which centuries spared,
  And at his frown they fade.

Yet sometimes in his withering path
  A lowly plant doth spring,
From seed of immortality
  That mocks his victor-sting.

In earth, in air, in ocean caves,
  All deprecate his wrath,
He crusheth thrones, yet fears to mow
  That balm-flower in his path.

The balm-flower that behind him grows,
  Wet with the mourner's tear,
That springs to staunch the bleeding heart,
  A Saviour standing near,

Strong faith, deep love, unfading trust,
  That deck the Christian's tomb,
Heaven's guerdon to the born of dust,—
  He dares not blight their bloom.

A TALK WITH THE BROOKS.

THE voice of brooks spake to me, as I walked
At winter noon-day. Up, through icy veils,
Cold and transparent, glanced their sparkling eyes,
While ever and anon, as some brief plunge
Gave them advantage o'er the softening banks,
They brake their fetters.

"Why have ye come forth
Thus, ere your time, to touch with trembling green
The taper grass-blades, and the tiny plants
That on your margin grow?"

"They slept so long,"
The brooklets said, "we feared they would forget
The mighty Quickener's name, who ever decks
This earth with beauty. So we gently waked
Their cradle-dream, bidding them learn of us
The Maker's praise, which, murmuring, we repeat."

"Make haste on your sweet errand, tuneful brooks!
Tint these young lips with life while yet ye may,
For, lo! stern Winter weaves a stronger chain
To bind ye, hand and foot. Methinks, I hear
Even now, his purpose, on the rising blast."

"Then," they replied, "our lesson is for man:
When God shall shut the storm-cloud o'er his joys,
And quell his song, let him bear on like us,
In meekness, and in hope."

AN OLD STORY.

SAYS Tom to Jem, as forth they went
  To walk one evening fine,
"I wish the sky a great green field,
  And all that pasture mine."

"And I," says Jem, "wish yonder stars,
  That there so idly shine,
Were every one a good fat ox,
  And all those oxen mine."

"Where would your herd of cattle graze?"
  "Why, in your pasture fair."
"They should not, that's a fact," said Tom;
  "They shall not, I declare!"

With that they frowned, and struck, and fought,
  And fiercely stood at bay,
And for a foolish fancy cast
  Their old regard away.

And many a war, on broader scale,
  Hath stained the earth with gore,
For castles in the air, that fell
  Before the strife was o'er.

THE LANDING OF THE PILGRIMS.

A PICTURE BY GEORGE FLAGG.

At prayer!—at prayer, upon the snow-clad rock,
The cold, bleak sky above them.
Holy man,—
Heart on thy lips, and Bible in thy hand,
Pour forth, as far as feeble speech may do,
The intense emotion of the gathered throng.

Rest on thy sword, thou man of blood,* and muse,
Thy fading Rose beside thee. Bow and ask
Strength for new warfare, when the savage foe
Shall plant his ambush, and the secret shaft
Ring through the forest, while the war-whoop wakes
The frighted infant, on its mother's breast.

Prithee, John Alden, say thy prayers with zeal,
Forgetful of thy comeliness, and her
Who Cupid's subtle snare shall weave for thee,
When, here and there, the settler's roofs shall mix
With the fresh verdure of this stranger soil.

* Miles Standish.

Oh, noble Carver! boundless is thy wealth,
In the pure heart that thus doth cling to thine,
With all the trustfulness of woman's love,
And all its firm endurance. He who boasts
Such comforter shall find the barren heath
Thick sown with flowers of Eden.
Pale, and sweet,
Ah! suffering bride of Winslow, 'tis in vain
That thus he fondly clasps thy fragile hand:
He may not guard thee from the ghastly foe
That on thy forehead stamps the seal of doom.
He cannot keep thee, lady. Snows may chill
Thy foot, that England's richest carpets prest,
A little while, and then the soul that sits
Bright on thine upraised eye, shall heavenward soar.

Oh lone and tiny May-Flower! ark that touched
Our Ararat, without a herald-dove
Or greeting leaf of olive,—speed thy course
Homeward in hope. For henceforth shalt thou be
Remembered through all time. Thou, who hast been
Seed-bearer for a nation, shalt be held
Right blessed for thy deed, and on the lip
Of each succeeding race, shalt freshly dwell
With holy memories of those pilgrim sires
Who taught New England's wilds Jehovah's name.

THE PRAYER ON BUNKER HILL.

During the battle of Bunker Hill, a venerable clergyman knelt on the field, with hands upraised, and gray head uncovered, and while the bullets whistled around him, prayed for the success of his compatriots, and the deliverance of his country.

IT was an hour of fear and dread—
High rose the battle-cry,
And round, in heavy volumes, spread
The war-cloud to the sky;
'Twas not, as when in rival strength
Contending nations meet,
Or love of conquest madly hurls
A monarch from his seat.

Yet one was there unused to tread
The path of mortal strife,
Who but the Saviour's flock had fed
Beside the fount of life;
He knelt him where the black smoke wreathed,
His head was bowed and bare,
While for an infant land he breathed
The agony of prayer.

The column, red with early morn,
  May tower o'er Bunker's height,
And proudly tell a race unborn
  Their patriot fathers' might;
But thou, O patriarch old and gray!
  The prophet of the free,
Who knelt among the dead that day—
  What fame shall rise to thee?

It is not meet that brass or stone,
  Which feel the touch of time,
Should keep the record of a faith
  That makes thy deed sublime;
We trace it on a tablet fair,
  Which glows when stars wax pale—
A promise that the good man's prayer
  Shall with his God prevail.

POWERS'S STATUE OF THE GREEK SLAVE.

Be silent! breathe not! lest ye break the trance;
She thinketh of her Attic home; the leaves
Of its green olives stir within her soul,
And Love is sweeping o'er its deepest chords
So mournfully. Ah! who can weigh the wo
Or wealth of memory in that breast sublime!

Yet errs he not who calleth thee *a slave*,
Thou Christian maiden?
Gyves are on thy wrists;
But in thy soul a might of sanctity
That foils the oppressor, making to itself
A hiding-place from the sore ills of time.
What is the chain to thee, who hast the power
To bind in admiration all who gaze
Upon thine eloquent brow and matchless form?
We are ourselves thy slaves, most Beautiful!

APRIL.

Month of the smile and tear! Thou dost inherit
  A losing gift from thy precursor's hand,
An unquenched feud, sustained with lion spirit
  Against stern Winter, and his ruffian band;
  The stormy March, whose quarrels shook the land,
Left but sad legacy to thee, I ween,
  Who, like a girl, all moved to laughter bland,
Must gird thy tender limbs in armour sheen,
And battle for thy rights upon the changeful green.

And hark! the northern winds, thine angry foes
  Sweep from their mountain-towers, like barons bold,
While, in their secret nooks, the cunning snows
  Intrench themselves, resolved with durance cold
  Possession for their exiled king to hold;
But the slant sunbeams waste them day by day,
  And through their breasts, with arrogance untold
The wily brooklets mine their murmuring way,
And 'neath the fretted arch, a thousand gambols play.

Yet doth thy soft hand claim the victory,
Month of the smile and tear! for here and there,
The infant grass-blades peering toward the sky
Win that green tint which maketh earth so fair,
And many a bulb, that by the florist's care
Found pillow warm beneath the sheltering ground,
And many a hardy bud, the blasts that dare,
Have heard God's voice amid the garden's bound,
And from their cradles looked and listened to the sound.

They listen, they unfold, to life they spring,
The pallid snow-drop at the violet's feet,—
The young arbutus, with its glossy wing
Shadowing its forehead,—on her queenly seat
The hyacinth, dispensing perfume sweet,
The fairy crocus, all in haste arrayed,
The simple daisy, with the cowslip sweet,
Have heard God's voice amid the garden glade,
Yet not, like Eden's pair, with conscious guilt afraid.

Month of the smile and tear! Thy mild behest
A countless band of choristers await:
The soaring lark unloads his warbling breast,
The thrush melodious woos his gentle mate,
The chirping robin at the cottage-gate
Partakes his crumbs, and with a song repays;

Up goes the oriole, bright in kingly state:
God's voice they hear, with true responsive lays,
Nor like our ingrate hearts, forego the debt of praise.

Nature, all beauteous in the garb of Spring,
Thou, as a goddess to her temple-shrine,
With budding wreaths and chant of birds dost bring;
And there, with breathing eloquence divine,
Whether in hymns, where woods and waters join,
Or solemn sounds, when sky-crowned forests nod
Or spirit-voices, low at eve's decline,
When the lone lily trembleth on the sod,
She doth announce herself a Teacher sent from God.

The world hath other lessons, other charms,
To stir the selfish passions. Lust of fame
Goads the stern warrior on to deeds of arms;
Wealth o'er the crowd maintains a golden claim;
The mournful odour of a mangled name
Lures Slander's harpies, posting on the wind:
Even cloistered Learning feeds Contention's flame;
But Nature—holy nurse of human kind—
Back to its Glorious Sire doth lead the ethereal mind.

DIVINE WISDOM.

Temporal afflictions sometimes hide those eternal blessings to which they lead; as temporal enjoyments cover those eternal evils which they too often procure."

PASCAL.

GOD'S will, God's will, my soul! and not thine own,
No, not thine own!
Thou hadst an earnest choice
To look on pleasant things beneath the sun,
Sweet flowers and fruitful vines; but most of all
To taste that love which bindeth heart to heart,
In close communion.
But thy choice was made
In darkness, and thou know'st not what was best:
He knoweth,—the Eternal!
They who hoard
Metallic heaps, say, what will that avail
When from their death-struck hands the gold shall fall,
O'er selfish, thankless, or estranged hearts,
While they, amid the tossings of disease,
Part to return no more?

And they who make
Ambition master, and his bidding do,
Upon the war-cloud, trampling fiercely down
All loves, all charities, all bonds of right,
And bringing plagues upon the souls of men,
That they may swell in greatness,—is their gain
A blessing, or a pang, when they shall tread
That lone St. Helena, which conscience makes,
And wrestle with the death-pang, unsustained
By breath of treacherous fame?
Even they, who reap
The fulness of their hope in earthly love,
Finding each sorrow lulled by sympathy,
Each joy reflected from the mirror-plate
Of a quick, answering heart, do they repose
Too fondly on their idols?—Do they claim
Firm property in that which is but dust,
And so complain, when on the winged winds,
Uplifted lightly, it doth fleet away?
Doth Heaven's rich bounty make the erring heart
Shrink from the travel of eternity?
It may be so—and therefore He who knows
Our frame hath gathered round this banquet-board
The hyssop branch and taste of bitter herbs,
And where we grasp a rose-wreath, as we think,—
Gives us a thorn to kiss.

Yes, and He sends
Deep voices to us, from the Spirit-Land,
Breathed from the lips that once on earth were dear,
And tenderly they teach us how to strike
The key-note of that never ending song,
Which through the arch of heaven's high temple swells,
"God's will, not ours!—God's praise forever more!"

THE LAST JOURNEY OF HENRY CLAY.

He passeth on his way,
  The man to senates dear,
The silver-voiced, whom gathered throngs
  Still held their breath to hear.
He hath no warrior's crown,
  No laurel on his breast,
But Peace her drooping olive binds
  Amid his stainless crest.

He shrank not at his post
  Till the spoiler grasped his hand,
And sternly chained the silver tongue
  Whose music charmed the land.
Mid Summer's glorious pride
  With the tramp of an iron steed,
He sweepeth on, o'er the realm he loved—
  But his closed eye takes no heed.

Our cities veiled their heads
 As through their gates he passed,
And the mournful voice of tolling bells
 Wailed out upon the blast:
And forth our noblest came
 To guard their sacred trust,
And weeping woman cast her wreath
 Upon his honoured dust.

He passeth on his way
 In more than kingly state,
And silent children press to gaze
 Upon the fallen great;
While from the ramparts proud,
 Where his country's banners fly,
The booming cannon speaks his praise—
 But he deigneth no reply.

There's sorrow on the wave
 As the coffined dead they bring—
The passing ships their pennons furl,
 Like an eagle's broken wing;
And as the rippling streams
 That precious burden bore,
The murmuring rivers tell their grief
 To every shrouded shore.

He passeth on his way,
  To his own cultured lawn—
The shadow of his planted trees
  That bloom when he is gone:
And agonizing love
  Beholds with stifled moan,
A nation's tear upon the bier,
  That mingles with her own.

Bow down in reverent wo
  Beside his sable pall,
The friend of man, who fearless sought
  The brotherhood of all!
Strong in a Saviour's strength
  When life's frail web was riven,
The Truth and Peace he loved on earth
  Made him at home in Heaven.

FRIENDSHIP WITH NATURE.

Benighted wanderer o'er the lonely wild,
For whom no hearth-stone blazes, no fond eye
Watches through gathering mist—no voice of love
Prepares the welcome greeting—droop not thus,
Disquieted and desolate. Look up!
Orion holds his golden lamp for thee;
And see, from highest heaven, the kingly orb
Of Sirius doth thee honour with its beam,
Yea, even the fair-robed queenly moon doth bow
Upon her silver throne, to guide thy feet
Mid thorns and pitfalls.

Dost thou mourn to feel
Forgotten here, upon this little point
Of one small planet? Lo! majestic worlds,
That turning on their glowing axles, hide
The mysteries of their myriad habitants,
Smile on thee, full of friendly offices,
Making night's vault for thee most beautiful

With their bright tokens. And the glorious sun,
Chief of God's creatures in our universe,
Shall wake to give thee light, as cheerily
As to the proudest king.
So, be not sad!
If mortals scorn thee, fly to Nature's arms
And ever open breast. For he who lives
Nearest to her, is never far from God.
Yes, make of Nature an enduring friend,
That when grim Age shall lay his hand on thee,
Plucking thee bare of all the cherished plumes
Of youth and fancy, every wild-winged bird
Cleaving the air, or brooding o'er its nest
With soul-born music, every bud that lifts
Its infant chalice, full of morning dew,
May touch the fountains of remembered joy,
Making thee young again.
And when at last
The dark death-angel cometh, earth shall ope
Her mourning matron breast, more tenderly,
More full of grief, than when the haughty chief,
With blood-stained laurels and proud funeral train,
Lies down to be forgotten.
She shall make
Thy chamber in the dust, and spread thy couch,
And bid the grass-flower and the violet

Embroider its green turf, as daintily
As though the clarion-cry of wealth and fame
Had proudly heralded thy pilgrimage.
Regard not Time's brief tyranny, oh, man!
Made in God's image—but uplift thy brow,
And by the glory of the inward light
Which falls on Nature's dial night and day,
Mark out thy journey to the realm of love.

"I STILL LIVE."

THE LAST WORDS OF DANIEL WEBSTER.

"*Still I live!*" The leaves were falling
Round the mansion where he lay,
And autumnal voices calling,
Warned the summer's pride away,
While the sighing surge of ocean,
In its crested beauty ran,
Breaking with a ceaseless motion,
Like the fleeting hopes of man.

"*Still I live!*" Oh, strong and glorious
Were those prophet words of cheer;
For where'er in truth victorious,
Greatness hath its worship here,
Patriot power its high ovation,
Eloquence its lofty birth,
He shall win from every nation,
An undying name on earth.

"*Still I live!*" The flesh was failing,
  All in vain the healer's skill,
Light in that deep eye was paling,
  And the mighty heart grew still:—
Yet the soul, its God adoring,
  Clad in armour firm and bright,
O'er the body's ruin soaring,
  Mingled with the Infinite.

Where he sleeps, that man of glory,
  Marshfield's mournful shades can say,
And his weeping country's story
  Darkened on that funeral day;
But the love that deepest listened,
  Caught such balm as Heaven can give,
For an angel's pinion glistened
  At the echo—"*Still I live!*"

GOD SAVE THE PLOUGH

SEE,—how the shining share
Maketh earth's bosom fair,
    Crowning her brow,—
Bread in its furrow springs,
Health and repose it brings,
Treasures unknown to kings,
    God save the plough!

Look to the warrior's blade,
While o'er the tented glade,
    Hate breathes his vow,—
Strife its unsheathing wakes,
Love at its lightning quakes,
Weeping and wo it makes,
    God save the plough!

Ships o'er the deep may ride,
Storms wreck their banner'd pride,
    Waves whelm their prow,

But the well-loaded wain
Garnereth the golden grain,
Gladdening the household train,
God save the plough!

Who are the truly great?
Minions of pomp and state,
Where the crowd bow?
Give us hard hands and free,
Culturers of field and tree,
Best friends of liberty—
God save the plough!

THE TEACHER.

To teach the young, and walk at shining morn,
Mid the pure air, and Nature's harmonies
Of bird or stream, unto the work that gives
The light of knowledge to the grateful mind,
And, at the close of day, to homeward turn
For the sweet rest that diligence deserves,
And self-approval cheers, is less a toil
Than privilege.
But the intenser care
That hath no interval, of him who shares
His roof-tree with his pupils, and beholds,
Both at uprising and retiring hours,
At board and fireside, their observant glance
Ever upon him, needeth full supplies
Of grace divine. Yea, almost might he ask
An angel's wisdom, lest infirmity

Or inadvertence, in those household hours
When men unbend, should mar authority.—
Still, if in tenderness of heart he strives
To view them as his children, and to bear
With martyr's patience, and to extirpate
As conscience prompts, and to hope on when hope
Seems dead, yet not for lucre's sake alone
But "ever in the Great Taskmaster's eye,"—
Doubtless he'll reap a harvest, either here
Or in the better land.
Let such be praised,
And held in honour. For they do the work
Deputed to the parent, unsutained
By that rich filial love, whose sweetness makes
All burdens light. And I have seen such care
Crowned with enduring gratitude, though oft
The boy, unskilled to read the motive right
That curbs a wayward impulse, doth mistake
Justice for tyranny, and so revolt,
Darkening the promise of his early years.

Yet many a germ of tenderness hath birth
From this familiar intercourse, that bears
In young and generous natures, blessed fruit
Of friendship for the Teacher, such as time
And hoary hairs impair not.

Once I saw
A nursery for the mind, 'mid rural shades
Pleasantly wrapped, remote from tempting snares,
Or interrupting sounds of city life.
Within its walls a spacious garden spread,
Where each a little space might call his own,
And stock as best he pleased, with fruit or flower,
Berry or salad. From an orchard near
The ripening apples told of luscious treat
At lengthened eve, which all should freely share.
Forest and dale around gave fitting room
For summer ramble, and the icy pool
Responsive rang beneath the skater's heel.
These were for hours of sport, but 'neath the roof
Study and discipline, with earnest sway
Enforced their claims.
One morn, a fair-haired lad
Brought to the master's desk a folded note,
Of neat chirography, in ardent phrase
Asking a holiday.
The wintry storm
Had long been raging, smiting, night and day,
The moaning evergreens; but now the sun
Cast o'er the clear cold vault of sparkling blue
A compensating smile. Thus inly cheered
And strengthened by the coming of a guest

Honoured by all, who to the master paid
Brief visit, they adventured their request,
Unamimously signed.
The teacher's heart
Yearned to indulge them. But with features grave
And policy of pausing speech, he asked
Each how his lessons fared, intent to make,
If possible, the favour a reward;
Or else demurring conscience satisfy
With promises of better things to come,
Which many a young and fervent lip pronounced
Right heartily. So, with paternal smile
The boon he granted.
Who the joy can tell,
Unless the boyish nature he partake,
That with electric flash, from heart to heart
Thrilled at that lauded word.
With buoyant step
The glad group gathered. Some their rout disclosed
To a bold mount, whose palisaded head
Mixed in dim distance with a silvery cloud,
Intent to glean its crystals, and enrich
Their cabinets with fossils.
Some, alas!
With gun or belted quiver, told too plain
Their hostile purpose 'gainst the sylvan spoil.

To them the observant dog delighted hung,
And at each summons frisked with wilder zeal.
Some to the saddle sprang, while others sped
The rolling wheel to reach the neighbouring town,
And make the heart of friend or parent leap
At their bright, brief "*good-morrow.*"
Here and there
Amid the brisk pedestrian throng were seen
The osier basket, ominous of good,
Well by the matron's liberal kindness stored;
While ruddy fruit, from pocket peeping forth,
Bespoke wise forethought for the coming meal.
Even humbler creatures seemed to share the joy,
And quick from perch to perch the imprisoned bird
Flitted with outspread wing, while shriller tones
Gave vent to its impassioned melody.

Then, at the chosen leader's bugle call,
The exploring troop set forth, as full of glee
As sport, and the elastic play of limbs,
And the free spirit of the woods could make
The healthful heart. Would that the pensive eye
Of many a distant mother now might glance
Upon her graceful and glad-hearted boy

For whom so oft it gusheth in the prayer
That hath no words.
Oh teacher! it is well
To mingle sunbeams with the seed that sows
The immortal mind. Damp sorrow's moody mist
Doth quell the aspiring thought, and steal away
Childhood's young wealth of happiness, that God
Gave as its birthright. Strive to blend the glow
Of gladness with thy discipline, and urge
Duty by love. Remember how the blood
Coursed through thine own quick veins, when life was new,
Nor make the isthmus 'tween the boy and man
A bridge of sighs.

THE PLANT AT SEA.

Hold up thy head, thou timid voyager!
  Vexed by the storm-clouds as they darkly roll,
And by those fiercely tossing waves that stir
  Thy slender root, and try thy trembling soul.

Sad change from that sweet garden, where the dew
  Each morning glistened in thy grateful eye,
And where the roughest guest thy bosom knew
  Was earnest bee, or gadding butterfly.

It grieves me sore to see thy leaflets fade,
  Wearing the plague-spot of the chilling spray,
And know what trouble I for thee have made:
  Yet still bear on, meek partner of my way,

For in thy tender life I hold the chain
Of home and its delights, here on the lonely main.

MORNING, IN RURAL AND CITY LIFE.

"God made the country, and man made the town."—COWPER.

MORN breaketh on the mountains. Their gray peaks
Catch its first tint, and through the mist that veils
Their rugged foreheads, smile, as when the stars
Together sang, at young Creation's birth.
——Fresh gales awake, and the tall pines bow down
To their soft visit, and the umbrageous oaks
Spread their broad banner, while each leaf doth lift
Itself, as for a blessing. Through the boughs
Of the cool poplars, steals a sighing sound,
The leaping rills make music, and the groves
Pour, from their cloistered nests, a warbling hymn.—
While earth, and air, and Nature's varied voice,
Like the clear horn amid the Alpine hills,
Is praise to God, at this blest hour of morn.

——Morn cometh to the cottage. Through its door
Peep ruddy faces. Infant mirth awakes,
The fair, young milk-maid o'er the threshold trips,

The shepherd's dog goes forth, the lamb sports gay,
And the swain dips his glittering scythe in dew,
Which, like bright tears, the new shorn grass hath shed.
Joy breathes around, while Health, with glowing lips
And cheek embrowned, and Industry with song
Of jocund chorus, hail the King of Day.

——Morn is upon the city. See, how slow
Its ponderous limbs unfold. On arid sands
Thus the gorged boa, from some dire repast,
Uncoils his length. Heaven smileth on those spires;
Yet their loud bells, and organ pipes, and hymns
Of high response, are silent. Flame hath fallen
Wherewith to kindle incense; still man locks
His bosom's altar, and doth sell for sleep,
What Esau sold for pottage. Lordly domes
And marble columns proudly greet the sun,
But not, like Memnon's statue, utter forth
A gratulating tone.
                    Aurora comes
Lightly pavilioned on a purple cloud;—
Sworn worshippers of beauty—where are ye?
Look!—Egypt's queen came not so daintily,
When on the Cydnus her resplendent barge
Left golden traces. But your eyes, perchance,

Are dim with splendors of some midnight hall,
And plunged in down, forego this glorious sight.

——Hark! life doth stir itself. The dray-horse strikes
His clattering hoof, eyeing with quivering limb
The tyrant-lash. And there are wakeful eyes
That watched for dawn, where sickness holds its sway,
Marking with groans the dial-face of Time.—
Half-famished Penury from its vigil creeps,
The money-seeker to his labour goes,
Gaunt Avarice prowls—but where are Wealth and Power—
The much-indebted, and the high-endowed?
Count they heaven's gifts so carelessly, that Morn
With glowing blush, may claim no gratitude?
Lo! from their plenitude Disease hath sprung—
The dire disease that ossifies the heart,
And Luxury enchains them, when the soul
With her fresh, waking pulse should worship God.

GREGORY BRANDON.

[Gregory Brandon, the executioner of Charles the First, did not long survive him, and pined in his last sickness for want of the forgiveness of his sovereign.]

"WHAT irks thee, father?—in thy sleep
I see thee toss and start,
While sometimes deep and fearful groans
Burst from thy labouring heart,
And often, since this fever came,
I hear thee wildly say,
Amid the conflict of thy dream,
'*Turn, turn those eyes away.*'"

"My life hath been a life of blood,"
The sick man said with pain,
"And monsters from its curdling flood
Creep out and haunt my brain:
But, daughter, such hath been thy love,
That I will tell thee true."
He paused, and o'er his forehead came
The starting drops, like dew.

"When civil war, with countless ills,
  Our suffering land dismayed,
I still was reckless of her woe,
  Nor loathed the headman's trade.
Full many a proud and gallant head
  My axe hath shred away,
And merry was I in my cups,
  Though I had need to pray.

"Once, on a bitter, wintry day,
  Five weeks from Christmas tide,
When in Rosemary Lane we lived,
  Ere your poor mother died,
Stout Axtel drew me from my home,
  Stern man he was, and grim,
And, with a heavy, silver bribe
  Lured me to go with him.

"A butcher's coat, a sable mask,
  Did form and face enshrine,
And well such hideous garb beseemed
  So dire a deed as mine,
To Whitehall's stately dome he led,
  And by that palace fair,
Strange guest!—a scaffold rudely framed,
  And block, and axe, were there.

"Then, from that fair and princely hall,
  Where oft the feast was spread,
He came,—who bare the anointing oil
  Upon his royal head,
As noble was his beaming brow,
  As clear his dauntless tone,
As when a sceptred hand he raised,
  And filled a nation's throne.

"None, save a prelate bathed in tears,
  A servant true and tried,
A soldier with uncovered head,
  Stood firmly by his side;*
While all around, a countless throng
  Like blackening clouds did lower,
That erst with peans loud and long
  Would hail his day of power.

"The hour had come, I bowed me down
  There, on that fatal spot,
To win his pardon for my crime;
  Yet he forgave me not,

---

* Bishop Juxon, Sir Thomas Herbert, and Col. Tomlinson, accompanied Charles the First to the scaffold.

But turned his large and lustrous eyes
With such a mournful ray,
That never from my inmost soul
Their glance hath fled away.

"The hour had come. The prelate spake
Like one with anguish riven:
'One stage alone, my king, remains,
One step from earth to heaven.'
Calm was the sufferer's voice, 'A clime
From all disturbance free,
A heavenly and immortal crown
A good exchange shall be.'

"He murmured low, in prayer profound,
Beside the block he knelt;
But ah! once more those searching eyes
Did make my spirit melt.
And scarcely knowing what I did,
I struck!—with hollow sound
Methought the moaning earth replied,—
And all was dark around.

"I saw not, when that head they raised;
Yet on the scaffold dire,

The trickling drops of sacred blood
  Did scathe my soul like fire,
While from the people's grieving heart
  Rose such a groan of pain,*
As never more this English realm
  I trust shall hear again.

"Then fiercely through the mourning ranks
  The armėd horsemen rode,
Rudely enforcing every man
  To seek his own abode;
But there in mine, my glittering hoard,
  My thirty pounds well told,

---

* The biographer of the Rev. Philip Henry, a pious and excellent non-conformist divine, thus remarks: "He was at Whitehall, January 30th, 1648, when the king was beheaded, and with a sad heart saw that tragical blow given. Two things he used to speak of, which I know not whether any of the historians mention. One was, that, at the instant when the blow was given, there was such a dismal, universal groan among the many thousands of people, as he never heard before, and desired he might never hear the like again. The other was, that, immediately after the stroke was struck, there was, according to order, one troop marching from Charing Cross towards King-street, and another from King-street to Charing Cross, purposely to disperse and scatter the people, and divert the dismal thoughts that they could not but be filled with, by driving them to shift every one for his own safety,"

Seemed as the traitor Judas' hire,
For which his hope was sold."

"O father! father! fret not so,"
The pitying maiden said,
"It was your lot, and not your will,
To do this work of dread.
Grim men were those, and hard of heart,
Who bore the rule that day;
And had you spared the precious blood,
Most sure your own would pay."

"They might have torn me limb from limb,
Or crushed me to the tomb,
But thus to linger slow away
Doth seem a harder doom,—
To moulder piecemeal here, my child,
And night and day to see
Those solemn and reproachful eyes
For ever fixed on me.

"In health, or youthful prime, our sins
Lie on the conscience light;
But in the dark and evil time,
With scorpion lash they smite.

O daughter! who with duteous feet
  Life's dangerous path dost tread,
Keep clean thy hands, keep pure thy heart,
  And bide the bar of dread."

Once, at the chill and shadowy dawn,
  With noiseless step she crept
Beside the sick man's bed to see
  If peacefully he slept.
The straining eyes were open wide,
  The lips asunder set,
And closely clenched the wasted hands,
  As if some foe he met.

But in those orbs there was no light,
  Upon those lips no breath,
And every rigid feature wore
  The torture stamp of death.
And ever as she onward fared,
  Through change and chance of life,
Or wrote new titles on its scroll,
  Of mother and of wife,—

Oft, o'er her weary couch of rest,
  The dying sire would seem

With fixed and glazing eyes to give
  Strange horror to her dream.
And as the sinful wail arose
  Of one who shunned to pray,
She shuddered at the spirit-cry,—
  "*Turn, turn those eyes away.*"

THE DEPARTED YEAR.

SILENT and solemn pass the bannered hours,
As to a chieftain's funeral.
With sad brow,
And arms reversed, they hush their muffled tread,
Waiting the last toll of the midnight clock,
Then lift him from his hearse and lay him down
In the dark grave with such a mournful dirge,
Mid the red torches' glare, that he who heard
Shall ne'er forget again.
Departed year!
Thou hast had fitting obsequy, as one
Worthy to be remembered; yet what hand
Can write thine epitaph?
Thou hast induced
Changes on this, our little, restless ball
Of dust and ashes, that grave History
Starts as she chronicles. They who could put
Their voice into men's souls and stir them up

Till nations trembled, have fallen down to sleep,
Weak as the smitten babe.
New thrones have sprung
Forth from the seething ruins of the past,
With blood and fire around them.
O'er the floods
Men speed like winds, and o'er the earth like flames,
And launch their errands on the lightening's wing,
Making its shaft a spear-point, at their will
To pierce the dinted target where old Time
Notched his slow victories.
Thou hast achieved
Much ere thy course was run. But thou art gone
With buried ages to hold festival
In the dim, shadowy halls, where ghostly things
Wait the slow verdict of posterity.
Men, fallible, and girt with prejudice,
Pass sentence as they list; but as for us,
Whom on our journey to a land unknown
Thou didst set forward duly, night and day,
We shall have righteous judgment from high Heaven
Concerning all our intercourse with thee.

MONODY TO DANIEL WADSWORTH.

Thou, of an honoured name,
That gave in days of old,
Shepherds to Zion's fold,
And chiefs of power and fame,
When Washington, in times of peril drew
Forth in their country's cause, the valiant and the true,
Thou, who so many a lowly home didst cheer,
Counting thy wealth a sacred trust,
With shuddering heart the knell we hear
That tells us, thou art dust.

Friend! we have let thee fall
Into the grave and have not gathered all
The wisdom thou didst love to pour
From a rich mind's exhaustless store;
Ah! we were slow of heart
To reap the ripened moments ere their flight,
Or thou, perchance, to us hadst taught the art
Heaven's gifts to use aright;
Amid infirmity and pain
Time's golden sands to save;

With steadfast heart the truth maintain;
To frown on ills the life that stain,
Making the soul their slave;
To joy in all things beautiful, and trace
The slightest smile or shade, that mantled nature's face.

Yes, we were slow of heart, and dreamed
To see thee still at evening-tide
With page of knowledge spread, thy pleasant hearth beside,
When to thy clearer sight there gleamed
The beckoning hand, the waiting eye,
The smile of welcome from the sky,
Of *Her* who was thine Angel here below,
And unto whom 'twas meet that thou shouldst long to go.

Friend! thou didst give command
To him who dealt thy soul its heavenly bread,
As by thy suffering bed
He took his faithful stand,
Not to pronounce thy praise, when thou wert dead;
So, though impulsive promptings came
Warm o'er his lips, like rushing flame,
He struggled, and o'ercame;
Even when in sad array
From thy lone home, where summer roses twined,
The weepers listened ere they took their way

In funeral ranks, thy sable hearse behind,
And 'neath the hallowed dome, where thou so long
Hadst meekly worshipped with the Sabbath throng,
Thy venerated form was laid,
While mournful dirges rose and solemn prayers were made.

Oh Friend! thou didst o'ermaster well
The pride of wealth, and multiply
Good deeds, not done for the good word of men
But for the Master's Eye,
And Heaven's recording pen,
For thou didst wisely weigh
Earth's loud applause and Fame's exulting swell,
Like bubble dancing on the noon-tide ray,
A sigh upon the grave,
Scarce stirring the frail flowers that o'er its surface wave.

Yet deem not, Friend revered!
Oblivion o'er thy name shall sweep,
For the fair halls that thou hast reared
Thy cherished image keep;
Yon fairy cottage, in its robe of flowers;
Those classic turrets* where the stranger strays
Mid works of pictured art, and scrolls of ancient days;

* The Wadsworth Athenеum at Hartford, Connecticut.

And that gray tower, on Monte Vidies crest,
Where mid Elysian haunts and bowers,
Thou didst rejoice to see all people blest;
These chronicle thy name,
And still, in many a darkened cot
Where penury holds its sway,
Thou hast a tear-embalmed fame
That may not quickly pass away,
Or lightly be forgot.

Yet, were all dumb beside,
The lyre that thou didst wake, the lone heart thou didst guide
From early youth, with fostering care,
Inciting still, to do, or bear,
As God's good-will might be;
These, may not in cold silence bide,
For were it so, the stones on which we tread
Would find a tongue to chide
Ingratitude so dread:—
No! till the last, faint gleam of memory's fires
On the worn altar of the heart expires,
Leave thou, the much indebted free
To speak what truth inspires,
And deeply mourn for thee.

THE MOTHER OF WOLFE.

A WHITE sail reached the Ocean Isle,
  That awes the subject sea,
And with electric touch awoke
  Wild shouts of victory.

"Quebec is ours!—Montcalm is down!—
  The lilied flag is low!
The Plains of Abraham all are strewn
  With the defeated foe,

"There lie the men of France beside
  Their Indian allies base;
Our colonists like lions fought,
  And proved their Saxon race."

But ah! the sequel of the tale!—
  Must the sad truth be said,
That Wolfe, Britannia's hero brave,
  Is with the silent dead?

In tones of murmured grief they tell
  How wound on wound he bore,
Yet dauntless ruled the battle tide
  On that far, rocky shore.

Until the fatal shaft was sped,
  That sealed his ardent eye,
And, mid the trance of death, he caught
  The sound,—"They fly! they fly!"

"*Who fly?*"—"*The French!*"—a glorious light
  His pallid brow o'erspread;
"*I die content;*"—the heart grew still,
  And he was of the dead.

Red bonfires blazed from cliff to vale,
  Glad bells their greeting gave;
The loud Te Deum richly swelled
  From many a hallowed nave,

While to St. Paul's the exulting king
  With long procession hied,
And Pitt, the lofty statesman, drank
  The cup of patriot pride.

Yet in one Kentish town alone
  No jocund peal was rung,
And sad the fallen victim's name
  Was breathed from every tongue.

For there a lonely woman bent
  O'er her last earthly trust,
And wept as only mothers weep
  When what they love is dust.

Her thoughts were of the infant head
  That in her breast would hide,
The boy's bright brow, the clustering curls,
  Her early matron pride,

The youthful smile, the sparkling eye,
  Her pulse to joy that stirred,
The manly arm that never more
  Her feeble form must gird,

The flowing blood, the shuddering pang,
  She might not staunch or share;
And all his laurels were forgot
  In that intense despair.

For her, even hardest hearts confessed
  Soft pity's tender tide,
And that poor widowed mother's grief
  Allayed a nation's pride.

THE MUSE.

They say that the cell of the poet should be
Like the breast of the shell that remembers the sea,
Quiet and still, save a murmuring sigh
Of the far-rolling wave to the summer-lit sky;
Tasteful and polished, as coralline bowers,
Remote from intrusion, and fragrant with flowers.

'Twould be beautiful, surely, but as for me,
Nothing like this I expect to see,
For I've written my poetry, sooth to say,
In the oddest of places, by night or by day,
Line by line, with a broken chain,
Interrupted, and joined again.
I, if paper were wanting, or pencils had fled,
Some niche in the brain, spread a storehouse instead,
And Memory preserved, in her casket of thought,
The embryo rhymes, till the tablets were brought:

At home or abroad, on the land or the sea,—
Wherever it came, it was welcome to me.

When first it would steal o'er my infantine hour,
With a buz or a song, like a bee in a flower,
With its ringing rhythm, and its measured line,
What it was I could scarce divine,
Calling so oft, from my sports and play,
To some nook in the garden, away, away,
To a mound of turf which the daisies crown,
Or a vine-wreathed summer-house, old and brown,
On a lilac's green leaf, with a pin, to grave
The tinkling chime of the words it gave.

At dewy morn, when to school I hied,
Methought like a sister it went by my side,
Well pleased o'er the fresh lanes to gambol and stray,
Or gather the violets that grew by the way,
Or turn my lessons to rhyme, and bask
In a rose, 'till I finished my needle's task.

When Winter in frost did the landscape enfold,
And my own little study was cheerless and cold,
A humble resource from the exigence rose,
And a barn was my favourite place to compose;

For there I could stow myself snugly away,
With my pencil and slate, on a nice mow of hay;
While with motherly face peeping out from her rack,
The cow munched her food, with a calf at her back;
And the fancies that there in that solitude wrought,
Were as chainless and bright as the palace-born thought.

When school years were o'er, and the tremulous ray
Of the young dawn of life took the tinting of day,
With ardour and pride I delighted to share,
By the side of my mother, her sweet household care.
My callisthenics followed each morning, with zeal,
Were the duster and broom, and the great spinning-
wheel;
No curve of the spine in that region was feared,
And of nervous diseases we seldom had heard.
So, singing along, with a buoyant tread
I drew out a line, as I drew out a thread.
Bees and bluebirds the casement flew by,
Yet none were so busy or happy as I;
The voice of my wheel, like a harp in my ear,
And the Muse keeping time with her melody clear,
And the joy of my heart overflowing the lay,
And my parent's approval each toil to repay.

A season there was when the viol grew sweet,
And the maze of the dance was a charm to my feet,
For Youth and Joy, with their measures gay,
Beckoned me onward both night and day;
Yet oft in the soul was a secret tone
Winning away to my chamber lone,
And, lingering there, was a form serene
With a mild reproof on her pensive mien;
And though I feigned from her sway to start,
Having music enough in my own merry heart,
Yet her quiet tear on my brow that fell,
Was more dear than the dance or the viol's swell.

When life's mantling pleasures their climax attained,
And the sphere of a wife and a mother was gained,
When that transport awoke, which no language may
speak,
As the breath of my first-born stole soft o'er my cheek,
While she slept on my breast, in the nursery fair,
A smothered lyre would arrest me there,
Half complaining of deep neglect,
Half demanding its old respect;
And if I mingled its cadence mild
With the tuneful tones of the rosy child,
Methought 'twas no folly such garlands to twine,
As could brighten life's cares, and its pleasures refine.

And now, though my life from its zenith doth wane,
And the wreaths of its morning grow scentless and vain,
And many a friend who its pilgrimage blest,
Have fallen from my heart and gone down to their rest,
Yet still by my side, unforgetful and true,
Is the being that walked with me all the way through.
She doth cling to the High Rock wherein is my trust,
Let her chant to my soul when I go to the dust;
Hand in hand with the faith that my Saviour hath given
Let her kneel at His feet mid the anthems of Heaven.

LISTEN.

WILT be a listener?—not to tramp and shriek
Of the great iron steed that roams the world,
Nor to the jingle of the envied gold
That rules it,—these thou needst must hear perforce,
But wilt thou list to cadences that dwell
In hermit places and in noiseless hearts?

Nature hath secret lore for those who lean
Upon her breast, with leisure in their soul
To hear her voice. Birdlings and blossoms speak
Words understood by all, but unto him
Who puts the clamor of the crowd aside,
Weeds, and the rudest rocks give utterance
To melody and truth. Yea, the wide earth
Unfolds itself to his inquiring glance,
And to its humblest agents lends a voice
Of wisdom. Even the feeblest wave that breaks,
Casting the frailest shell upon the shore,

Hath pearls for him. He sees the spoonlike leaf
That thrusts itself from out the tropic plant,
Catch a bright rain-drop to make glad its root,
And win the mother-blessing. The pale flower
Braving the Alpine cliff, doth tell his soul
Of the kind angel that did nourish it.
Lo! occult Science, with her midnight lamp,
Demands the silence of a listening mind,
Refusing to be wooed by those who pour
Love songs to fancy, and shun solitude.
Inklings and guessings will not do for her,
My gay young student. She demandeth facts
Well followed out, and toils that give the mind
Sinew and muscle. From the mount she comes
Like Moses, with strange brightness on his face,
And in his hand the tablets of the skies,
Graven on stone, which in his wrath he brake,
To find a dancing people mad with mirth
Before their molten calf, who should have knelt
In awe-struck silence of humility,
To read the law by God's own finger traced.

Wilt listen to the heart? It hath a sigh
That the world heeds not, an inwoven mesh
Of hidden harp-strings. If thou'lt hold thy breath,
And with a meek and noiseless footstep, glide

Down the sad pathways of humanity,
Then shalt thou hear, from every passing breeze,
The sigh of souls that have no comforter,
Soft, echoed joys, as from a grass-bird's nest,
And broken strains of sublunary hope,
Till feeling in thyself the quickening tide
Of sympathy for all whom God hath made,
Thou lovest the Hand that rules these harmonies.

So listen, that the monotone of self
May die away, and with Creation's song,
Of many parts, thine own sweet praise ascend,
Until thou join the harpers round the throne.

THE THIRD DAY AT SEA.

THREE days at sea! The great-souled waves
  Have borne us on their crest,
And shrill-voiced winds from Eol's cave,
  Have piped us to our rest,
And as our ship, with foot of fire,
  Doth tread the surges cold,
And leave behind a glittering scroll,
  Like banner-staff unroll'd,
The mighty monsters of the main
  Pause in their boisterous play;
Or, glancing through the window'd brine,
  With terror haste away.

Three days at sea! I little thought
  'Twould be so hard to say
Farewell to home and cherished ones,
  And boldly launch away;

For from my childhood I had longed
  Through classic climes to rove,
Where yellow Tiber proudly rolls,
  Or Sappho sang of love,
Or where, o'er Snowden's forehead gushed,
  The Cambrian harp,—but tears
That round my hearth-stone rained that morn,
  Made dim the hope of years.

Three days! As long as he of old,
  The recreant prophet, staid
In living casket strangely sealed,
  Amid the sea-weed's shade;—
He, who from crime-stained Nineveh,
  Withheld the warning cry,
And in a ship of Tarshish thought
  To 'scape the all-seeing Eye,
And then, beside his smitten gourd,
  Spake out with murmuring breath,
To vindicate his bitter right
  Of anger unto death.

"*On the third day He rose.*" *Who rose?*
  My spirit's strength and stay;
Unto whose blessed skirts I'll cling
  Till life is rent away.

It matters not, though death draw nigh
  In curtained chamber fair,
Or on the deep, 'mid wrecking blasts,
  If He be with us there:
And may my ransomed soul at last,
  Time's storm-tried voyage o'er,
Sit down, like Mary, at his feet,
  And listen evermore.

ORISKA.

FAR in the west, where still the red man held
His rights unrifled, dwelt an aged chief,
With his young daughter. Joyous as a bird,
She found her pastime mid the forest shades,
Or with a graceful vigour urged her skiff
O'er the bright waters. The bold warriors mark'd
Her opening charms, but deem'd her still a child,
Or fear'd from their grave kingly chief to ask
The darling of his age.

A stranger came
To traffic with the people, and amass
Those costly furs which in his native clime
Transmute so well to gold. The blood of France
Was in his veins, and on his lips the wile
That wins the guileless heart. Ofttimes at eve
He sought the chieftain's dwelling, and allured

The gentle girl to listen to his tale,
Well framed and eloquent. With practised glance
He saw the love-flush on her olive cheek
Make answer to him, though the half-hid brow
Droop'd mid its wealth of tresses.
"Ah! I know
That thou dost love to please me. Thou hast put
Thy splendid coronet of feathers on.
How its rich crimson dazzles mid thy locks,
Black as the raven's wing! Thy bracelets, too!
Who told thee thou wert beautiful? Hast seen
Thy queenly features in yon mirror'd lake?
Bird of the Sioux! let my nest be thine,
And I will sing thee melodies that make
Midnight like morn."
With many a spell he charm'd
Her trusting innocence; the dance, the song,
The legend, and the lay of other lands;
And patient taught his pupil's lip to wind
The maze of words with which his native tongue
Refines the thought. The hoary chieftain frown'd;
But when the smooth Canadian press'd his suit
To be adopted by the tribe, and dwell
Among them, as a brother and a son,—
And when the indulgent sire observant read
The timid pleading of Oriska's eye,—

He gave her tenderly, with sacred rites,
In marriage to the stranger.
Their sweet bower
Rose like a gem amid the rural scene,
O'er-canopied with trees, where countless birds
Carol'd unwearied, the gay squirrel leap'd,
And the wild-bee went singing to his work,
Satiate with luxury. Through matted grass,
With silver foot, a frolic fountain stole,
Still track'd by deepening greenness, while afar
The mighty prairie met the bending skies,—
A sea at rest, whose sleeping waves were flowers.

Nor lack'd their lowly dwelling such device
Of comfort, or adornment, as the hand
Of gentle woman, sedulous to please,
Creates for him she loves. For she had hung
Attentive on his lips, while he described
The household policy of prouder climes;
And with such varied and inventive skill
Caught the suggestions of his taste refined,
That the red people, wondering as they gazed
On curtain'd window and on flower-crown'd vase,
Carpet and cushion'd chair, and board arranged
With care unwonted, call'd her home the court
Of their French princess.

A rich clustering vine
Crept o'er their porch, and 'neath its fragrant shade
Oriska sang her evening melodies,
Tuneful and clear and deep, the echoed truth
Of her soul's happiness. Her highest care
And dearest pleasure was to make his lot
Delightful to her lord; and he, well pleased
With the simplicity of fervent love,
And the high honour paid a chieftain's son,
Roam'd with the hunters at his will, or brought
Birdlings of brilliant plume, as trophies home
To his young bride.

Months fled, and with them change
Stole o'er his love. And when Oriska mark'd
The shadow darkening on his brow, she fear'd
The rudeness of her nation, or perchance
Her ignorance had err'd, and strove to do
His will more perfectly. And though his moods
Of harshness or disdain chill'd every joy,
She blamed him not, for unto her he seem'd
A higher being of a nobler race;
And she was proud and happy, might she bathe
His temples in some fit of transient pain,
Or by a menial's toil advance the feast
Which still she shared not. When his step was heard,
She bade her beating heart be still, and smooth'd

The shining tresses he was wont to praise,
And fondly hasting, raised her babe to meet
His father's eye, contented if the smile
That once was hers might beam upon his child:—
But that last solace fail'd, and the cold glance
Contemptuously repress'd her toil of love.
And then he came no more.

But as she watch'd
Night after night, and question'd every hour,
How bitterly those weeks and years were notch'd
Upon the broken tablet of the soul,
By that forsaken wife.

Calm moonlight touch'd
A fair Canadian landscape. Roof and spire,
And broad umbrageous tree, were saturate
With liquid lustre. O'er a lordly dome,
Whose halls had late with bridal pomp been gay,
The silvery curtains of the summer night
Were folded quietly.

A music-sound
Broke forth abruptly from its threshold stone,
Shrill and unearthly—not the serenade,
That thrills on beauty's ear, but a bold strain,
Loud even to dissonance, and oft prolonged
In low, deep cadence, wonderfully sad,—
The wild song of the Sioux. He who first

Awaking, caught that mournful melody,
Shudder'd with icy terror, as he threw
His mantle o'er him, and rush'd madly forth
Into the midnight air.
"Hence! Leave my door!
I know thee not, dark woman! Hence away!"

"Ah! let me hear that voice! How sweet its tones
Fall on my ear, although the words are stern.
Say! know'st thou not this boy? Whose eyes are these?
Those chestnut clusters round the lifted brow,—
Said'st thou not in his cradle they were thine?"

"How cam'st thou here, Oriska?"
"We have trod
A weary way. My father and his men
Came on the business of their tribe, and I,
Unto whose soul the midnight and the morn
Have been alike for years, roam'd restlessly
A wanderer in their train, leading our boy.
My highest hope was but to hear, perchance,
That thou didst live; and lo! a blessed guide
Hath shown me to thy home."
"Oriska, go!
I have a bride. Thou canst not enter here—
I'll come to thee to-morrow."

"*Wilt* thou come?
The white-hair'd chief, I fear me, fades away
Unto the Spirit-land!"
"I bid thee hence,
To thine abode. Have I not said to thee
I'll come to-morrow?"
With a heavy heart,
Through silent streets, the sad-brow'd woman went,
Leading her child.
Morn came, and day declined,
Yet still he came not. By her sire she watch'd,
O'er whose dull eye a filmy shadow stole,
While to her troubled question no reply
Rose from his palsied lip. Nature and age
Slept wearily and long. The second eve
Darken'd the skies, when lo! a well-known step—
He stood before her.
"Was it kind of thee,
Oriska, thus to break my bridal hour
With thy strange, savage music?"
"Was thy wife
Angry at the poor Indian? Not to speak
Harsh words I came: I would not think of thee
A thought of blame. But oh! mine aged sire,
Thou see'st him dying in this stranger-land,
Far from his fathers' graves. Be thou a friend

When he is gone and I am desolate.
Make me a household servant to thy wife.
I'll bring her water from the purest spring,
And plant the corn, and ply the flying oar,
And never be impatient or require
Payment from her, nor kind regard from thee.
I will not call thee husband,—though thou taught'st
My stammering lip that word when love was young,—
Nor ask one pitying look or favouring tone,
Or aught, except to serve and pray for thee
To the Great Spirit. And this boy shall do
Her will, and thine."
                                The pale face turn'd away
With well-dissembled anger, though remorse
Gnaw'd at his callous bosom!
                                        "Urge me not!
It cannot be!"
                        Even more he might have said,
Basely and bitterly, but lo! the chief
Cast off the ice of death, and on his bed,
With clenched hand and quivering lip, uprose:—

"*His* curse be on thee! He, who knoweth where
The lightnings hide!"
                                Around the old man's neck
Fond arms were wildly thrown. "Oh, curse him not!

The father of my boy." And blinding tears
Fell down so fast, she mark'd not with what haste
The white-brow'd recreant fled.

"I tell thee, child,
The cold black gall-drop in a traitor's soul
Doth make a curse. And though I curse him not,
The sun shall hate him, and the waters turn
To poison in his veins.

But light grows dim.
Go back to thine own people. Look no more
On him whom I have cursed, and lay my bones
Where my dead fathers sleep."

A hollow groan,
Wrung by extremest agony, broke forth
From the old chieftain's breast.

"Daughter, I go
To the Great Spirit."

O'er that breathless clay
Bow'd down the desolate woman. No complaint,
No sigh of grief burst forth. The tear went back
To its deep fountain. Lip and fringed lid
Trembled no more than in the statued bronze,
Nor shrank one truant nerve, as o'er her pass'd
The asphyxia of the heart.

Day after day,
O'er wild and tangled forest, moved a train,

Bearing with smitten hearts their fallen chief;
And next the bier a silent woman trod,
A child's young hand forever clasp'd in hers,
And on her lip no sound. Long was the way,
Ere the low roof-trees of their tribe they saw
Sprinkling the green; and loud the funeral wail
Rose for the honour'd dead, who, in his youth,
Their battles led, and in his wintry years
Had won that deeper reverence, which so well
The forest-sons might teach our wiser race
To pay to hoary age. Beneath the mounds,
Where slept his ancient sires, they laid him down;
And there the gather'd nation mourn'd their sire,
In the wild passion of untutor'd grief;
Then smoothed the pillow'd turf, and went their way.

Who is yon woman, in her dark canoe,
Who strangely towards Niagara's fearful gulf
Floats on unmoved?
Firm and erect she stands,
Clad in such bridal costume as befits
The daughter of a king. Tall, radiant plumes
Wave o'er her forehead, and the scarlet tinge
Of her embroider'd mantle, fleck'd with gold,
Dazzles amid the flood. Scarce heaves her breast,

As though the spirit of that dread abyss,
In terrible sublimity, had quell'd
All thought of earthly things.
Fast by her side
Stands a young, wondering boy, and from his lip,
Blanching with terror, steals the frequent cry
Of "Mother! Mother!"
But she answereth not.
She speaks no more to aught of earth, but pours
To the Great Spirit, fitfully and wild,
The death-song of her people. High it rose
Above the tumult of the tide that bore
The victims to their doom. The boy beheld
The strange, stern beauty in his mother's eye,
And held his breath for awe.
Her song grew faint,—
And as the rapids raised their whitening heads,
Casting her light oar to the infuriate tide,
She raised him in her arms, and clasp'd him close.
Then as the boat with arrowy swiftness drove
Down toward the unfathom'd gulf, while chilling spray
Rose up in blinding showers, he hid his head
Deep in the bosom that had nurtured him,
With a low, stifled sob.
And thus they took
Their awful pathway to eternity.—

One ripple on the mighty river's brink,
Just where it, shuddering, makes its own dread plunge,
And at the foot of that most dire abyss
One gleam of flitting robe and raven tress
And feathery coronet—and all was o'er,
Save the deep thunder of the eternal surge
Sounding their epitaph!

THE RETURN OF NAPOLEON

FROM ST. HELENA.

Ho! City of the gay!
  Paris! what festal rite
Doth call thy thronging million forth,
  All eager for the sight?
Thy soldiers line the streets
  In fix'd and stern array,
With buckled helm and bayonet,
  As on the battle-day.

By square, and fountain side,
  Heads in dense masses rise,
And tower and battlement and tree
  Are studded thick with eyes.
Comes there some conqueror home
  In triumph from the fight,
With spoil and captives in his train,
  The trophies of his might?

The "Arc de Triomphe" glows!
  A martial host are nigh,
France pours in long succession forth
  Her pomp of chivalry.
No clarion marks their way,
  No victor trump is blown;
Why march they on so silently,
  Told by their tread alone?

Behold! in glittering show,
  A gorgeous car of state!
The white-plumed steeds, in cloth of gold,
  Bow down beneath its weight;
And the noble war-horse, led
  Caparison'd along,
Seems fiercely for his lord to ask,
  As his red eye scans the throng.

Who rideth on yon car?
  The incense flameth high,—
Comes there some demi-god of old?
  No answer!—No reply!
Who rideth on yon car?—
  No shout his minions raise,
But by a lofty chapel dome
  The muffled hero stays.

A king is standing there,
  And with uncover'd head
Receives him in the name of France:
  Receiveth whom?—*The dead!*
Was he not buried deep
  In island-cavern drear;
Girt by the sounding ocean surge?
  How came that sleeper here?

Was there no rest for him
  Beneath a peaceful pall,
That thus he brake his stony tomb,
  Ere the strong angel's call?
Hark! hark! the requiem swells,
  A deep, soul-thrilling strain!
An echo, never to be heard
  By mortal ear again.

A requiem for the chief,
  Whose fiat millions slew,
The soaring eagle of the Alps,
  The crush'd at Waterloo:—
The banish'd who return'd,
  The dead who rose again,
And rode in his shroud the billows proud
  To the sunny banks of Seine.

They laid him there in state,
That warrior strong and bold,
The imperial crown, with jewels bright,
Upon his ashes cold,
While round those columns proud
The blazon'd banners wave,
That on a hundred fields he won,
With the heart's-blood of the brave;

And sternly there kept guard
His veterans scarr'd and old,
Whose wounds of Lodi's cleaving bridge
Or purple Leipsic told.
Yes, there, with arms reversed,
Slow pacing, night and day,
Close watch beside the coffin kept
Those veterans grim and gray.

A cloud is on their brow,—
Is it sorrow for the dead?
Or memory of the fearful strife
Where their country's legions fled?
Of Borodino's blood?
Of Beresina's wail?
The horrors of that dire retreat,
Which turn'd old History pale?

A cloud is on their brow,—
  Is it sorrow for the dead?
Or a shuddering at the wintry shaft
  By Russian tempests sped?
Where countless mounds of snow
  Mark'd the poor conscripts' grave,
And, pierced by frost and famine, sank
  The bravest of the brave.

A thousand trembling lamps
  The gather'd darkness mock,
And velvet drapes his hearse, who died
  On bare Helena's rock;
And from the altar near,
  A never-ceasing hymn
Is lifted by the chanting priests
  Beside the taper dim.

Mysterious one, and proud!
  In the land where shadows reign,
Hast thou met the flocking ghosts of those
  Who at thy nod were slain?
Oh, when the cry of that spectral host
  Like a rushing blast shall be,
What will thine answer be to them?
  And what thy God's to thee?

Paris, Tuesday, Dec. 15, 1840.

UNSPOKEN LANGUAGE.

LANGUAGE is slow. The mastery of wants
Doth teach it to the infant, drop by drop,
As brooklets gather.

Years of studious toil
Unfold its classic labyrinths to the boy;
Perchance its idioms and its sequences
May wear the shadow of the lifted rod,
And every rule of syntax leave its tear
For Memory's tablet.

He who would acquire
The speech of many lands, must make the lamp
His friend at midnight, while his fellows sleep,
Bartering to dusty lexicons and tomes
The hour-glass of his life.

Yet, there's a lore,
Simple and sure, that asks no discipline
Of weary years,—the language of the soul,
Told through the eye.

The mother speaks it well

To the unfolding spirit of her babe,
The lover to the lady of his heart,
At the soft twilight hour, the parting soul
Unto the angels hovering o'er its couch,
With Heaven's high welcome.

Oft the stammering lip
Marreth the perfect thought, and the dull ear
Doth err in its more tortuous embassy;
But the heart's lightning hath no obstacle;
Quick glances, like the thrilling wires, transfuse
The telegraphic thought.

The wily tongue,
To achieve its purpose, may disguise itself,
Oft, 'neath a glozing mask; and written speech
Invoke the pomp of numbers to enrich
Its dialect; but this ambassador
From soul to sense may wear the plainest suit,—
Ebon or hazel, azure-tint or gray,
It matters not: the signet-ring of truth
Doth give him credence.—

Once, old Ocean raged;
And a vex'd ship, by maddening waves impell'd,
Rush'd on the breakers. Mid the wild turmoil
Of rock and wave, the trumpet-clang, and tramp
Of hurrying seamen, and the fearful shock
With which the all-astonish'd mind resigns

The hope of life, a mother with her babe
Sate in the cabin. He was all to her,
The sole companion of her watery way,
And nestling towards her bosom, raised his face
Upward to hers.
                    Her raven hair fell down
In masses o'er her shoulders, while her eyes
Fix'd with such deep intensity, that his
Absorb'd their rays of thought, and seem'd to draw
The soul mature, with all its burdening cares,
Its wondrous knowledge, and mysterious strength,
Into his baby-bosom.
                    Word nor sound
Pass'd 'tween that mother and her youngling child,—
Too young to syllable the simplest name,—
And yet, methought, they interchanged a vow
Calmly beneath the unfathomable deep
Together to go down, and that her arm
Should closely clasp him mid its coral caves.
The peril pass'd; but the deep eloquence
Of that communion might not be forgot.

A youth and maiden, on the banks of Tweed,
Roved, mid the vernal flowers. At distance rose
The towers of Abbotsford, among the trees,

Which he, the great magician, who at will
Could summon "spirits from the vasty deep,"
Had loved to plant.

Methought of him they spake,
Disporting in the fields of old romance
With Ivanhoe, or the proud knight who fell
At Flodden-field. Then, as the sun drew low,
They sate them down, where the fresh heather grew,
Listing, perchance, the descant of the birds,
Or ripple of the stream. The hazel eye
Of the young dweller 'neath the Eildon-Hills
Perused the fair one's brow, till o'er it stole
A deeper colouring than the rose-leaf tinge.
—Speech there was none, nor gesture, yet the depth
Of some unutter'd dialect did seem
Well understood by them. And so they rose,
And went their way.

There was a crowded kirk,
But not for Sabbath worship. With the train
Was more of mirth than might, perchance, beseem
Such sacred place. Wreaths too there were, and knots
Of marriage-favour, and a group that prest
Before the altar. And the trembling lip
Of that young white-robed bride, murmuring the vow
To love till death should part, interpreted

That strong and voiceless language of the eye
Upon the banks of Tweed.—
I had a friend
Beloved in halcyon days, whom stern disease
Smote ere her prime.
In curtain'd room she dwelt,
A lingerer, while each waning moon convey'd
Some treasured leaflet of our hope away.
The power that with the tissued lungs doth dwell,
Sweetly to wake the modulating lip,
Was broken,—but the violet-tinctured eye
Acquired new pathos.
When the life-tide crept
Cold through its channels, o'er her couch I bent.
There was no sound. But in the upraised glance
Her loving heart held converse, as with forms
Not of this outer world. Unearthly smiles
Gave earnest beauty to the pallid brow;
While ever and anon the emaciate hand
Spread its white fingers, as it fain would clasp
Some object hovering near.
The last faint tone
Was a fond sister's name, one o'er whose grave
The turf of years had gather'd. Was she there,—
That disembodied dear one? Did she give

The kiss of welcome to the occupant
Of her own infant cradle?
So 'twould seem.
But that fix'd eye no further answer deign'd,
Its earthly mission o'er. Henceforth it spake
The spirit-lore of immortality.

NO CONCEALMENT.

"There is nothing covered, that shall not be revealed; and hid, that shall not be known."

St. Matthew.

Think'st thou to be conceal'd, thou little stream!
  That through the lowly vale dost wind thy way,
Loving beneath the darkest arch to glide
  Of woven branches, blent with hillocks gray?
The mist doth track thee, and reveal thy course
  Unto the dawn, and a bright line of green
Tingeth thy marge, and the white flocks that haste
  At summer-noon, to drink thy crystal sheen,
Make plain thy wanderings to the eye of day;
  And then thy smiling answer to the moon,
Whose beams so freely on thy bosom sleep,
  Unfold thy secret, even to night's dull noon.
How couldst thou hope, in such a world as this,
To shroud thy gentle path of beauty and of bliss?

Think'st thou to be conceal'd, thou little seed!
  That in the bosom of the earth art cast,
And there, like cradled infant, sleep'st awhile,
  Unmoved by trampling storm, or thunder blast?
Thou bidest thy time, for herald spring shall come
  And wake thee, all unwilling as thou art,
Unhood thine eyes, unfold thy clasping sheath,
  And stir the languid pulses of thy heart.
The loving rains shall woo thee, and the dews
  Weep o'er thy bed, till, ere thou art aware,
Forth steals the tender leaf, the wiry stem,
  The trembling bud, the flower that scents the air;
And soon, to all, thy ripen'd fruitage tells
The evil or the good that in thy nature dwells.

Think'st thou to be conceal'd, thou little thought!
  That in the curtain'd chamber of the soul
Dost wrap thyself so close, and dream to do
  A hidden work? Look to the hues that roll
O'er the changed brow, the moving lip behold,
  Linking thee unto sound, the feet that run
Upon thine errands, and the deeds that stamp
  Thy likeness plain before the noonday sun.
Look to the pen that writes thy history down
  In those tremendous books that ne'er unclose

Until the Day of Doom; and blush to see
  How vain thy trust in darkness to repose,
Where all things tend to judgment. So beware,
Oh erring human heart, what thoughts thou lodgest there.

THE NEEDLE, PEN, AND SWORD.

WHAT hast thou seen, with thy shining eye,
  Thou Needle, so subtle and keen?—
"I have been in Paradise, stainless and fair,
And fitted the apron of fig-leaves there,
  To the form of its fallen queen.

"The mantles and wimples, the hoods and veils,
  That the belles of Judah wore,
When their haughty mien and their glance of fire
Enkindled the eloquent prophet's ire,
  I help'd to fashion of yore.

"The beaded belt of the Indian maid
  I have deck'd with as true a zeal
As the gorgeous ruff of the knight of old,
Or the monarch's mantle of purple and gold,
  Or the satrap's broider'd heel.

I have lent to Beauty new power to reign,
  At bridal and courtly hall,

Or wedded to Fashion, have help'd to bind
Those gossamer links, that the strongest mind
Have sometimes held in thrall.

"I have drawn a blood-drop, round and red,
From the finger small and white
Of the startled child, as she strove with care
Her doll to deck with some gewgaw rare,
But wept at my puncture bright.

"I have gazed on the mother's patient brow,
As my utmost speed she plied,
To shield from winter her children dear,
And the knell of midnight smote her ear,
While they slumber'd at her side.

"I have heard in the hut of the pining poor
The shivering inmate's sigh,
When faded the warmth of her last, faint brand,
As slow from her cold and clammy hand
She let me drop,—*to die!*"

What dost thou know, thou gray goose-quill?—
And methought, with a spasm of pride,
It sprang from the inkstand, and flutter'd in vain,

Its nib to free from the ebon stain,
As it fervently replied:

"*What do I know!*—Let the lover tell
When into his secret scroll
He poureth the breath of a magic lyre,
And traceth those mystical lines of fire
That move the maiden's soul.

"*What do I know!*—The wife can say,
As the leaden seasons move,
And over the ocean's wildest sway,
A blessed missive doth wend its way,
Inspired by a husband's love.

"Do ye doubt my power? Of the statesman ask,
Who buffets ambition's blast,—
Of the convict, who shrinks in his cell of care,
A flourish of mine hath sent him there,
And lock'd his fetters fast;

"And a flourish of mine can his prison ope,
From the gallows its victim save,
Break off the treaty that kings have bound,
Make the oath of a nation an empty sound,
And to liberty lead the slave.

"Say, what were History, so wise and old,
And Science that reads the sky?
Or how could Music its sweetness store,
Or Fancy and Fiction their treasures pour,
Or what were Poesy's heaven-taught lore,
Should the pen its aid deny?

"Oh, doubt if ye will, that the rose is fair,
That the planets pursue their way,
Go, question the fires of the noontide sun,
Or the countless streams that to ocean run,
But ask no more what the Pen hath done."
And it scornfully turn'd away.

What are thy deeds, thou fearful thing
By the lordly warrior's side?
And the Sword answer'd, stern and slow,
"The hearth-stone lone and the orphan know,
And the pale and widow'd bride.

"The shriek and the shroud of the battle-cloud,
And the field that doth reek below,
The wolf that laps where the gash is red,
And the vulture that tears ere the life hath fled,

And the prowling robber that strips the dead,
  And the foul hyena know.

"The rusted plough, and the seed unsown,
  And the grass that doth rankly grow
O'er the rotting limb, and the blood-pool dark,
Gaunt Famine that quenches life's lingering spark,
  And the black-wing'd Pestilence know.

"Death with the rush of his harpy-brood,
  Sad Earth in her pang and throe,
Demons that riot in slaughter and crime,
And the throng of the souls sent, before their time,
  To the bar of the judgment—know."

Then the terrible Sword to its sheath return'd,
  While the Needle sped on in peace,
But the Pen traced out from a Book sublime
The promise and pledge of that better time
  When the warfare of earth shall cease.

FRUITFUL AUTUMN.

Autumn grows pallid, and his bounteous course
Draws near its close, while with a feeble hand
He languidly divides to those around
The last love-tokens.
A few brilliant wreaths—
Woodbine and dahlia, tinged with berries red
And twined with night-shade, and those snowy orbs
That cluster mournful round their naked stems,
He gives the children, and to older friends
Pointeth the rich bequests of better days,
Full granaries teeming with the golden ear,
And o'er the fields the abundant stacks, where throng
The quiet flocks and herds.
Art satisfied,
Thou of the plough and spade? Full heir of all
The year's perfected bounty, dost forget
The bounteous season at whose voice the wain

Roll'd heavy from the harvest? Earth attests
His benefactions.

But behold he dies!
Winds sing his dirge, and the brown leaves bestrew
His pathway to the tomb. Mourning, they say,
"Remember how he clothed us in bright robes,
Crimson and gold, even as that Jewish king,
Who fell at Gilboa, deck'd with gorgeous pride
Fair Israel's daughters."

Then the grass-blades breathed
A lowly sound, which he who bow'd his ear
To their crisp foreheads, caught:—

"He spared us long,
Holding the frost-king back, that we might cheer
Man with our simple beauty. Not in wrath,
Like some who went before him, did he tread
Upon our frailty. So we give him thanks."

Then the glad birds, from their migration held
By his warm smile, pour'd forth their grateful strain:
"He gave us food, and with no stinted hand
Scatter'd the seeds that pleased our callow young.
And chained the howling blasts that ere the time
Were wont to drive us from our nests away.
For this we love him."

And the bees replied:—

"We love him also, for he spared the flowers."
And the brisk squirrel mid his hoarded nuts,
And the light cricket in its evening song,
Yea, the poor gadding house-fly on the wall
Pronounced him pitiful and kind to them.

So, genial autumn, in thy grave with tears,
As when a good man dies, we lay thee down,
Covering thee with the verdure thou hast spared,
Fresh sods and lingering flowers.
Thou didst not trust
Thy purposed goodness to another's hand,
Cheating thy soul of the sweet bliss that flows
From pure philanthropy, but day by day
Aroused the labourer to his harvest-song,
Gladdening the gleaner's heart, and o'er the board
Of the poor man pouring such fruits as make
His meagre children happy.
Thus like thine,
Friend whom we praise, may our own course be found,
Not coldly trusting to a future race
Our plans of charity to execute,
When we are gone; but marking every hour
With some new deed of mercy, may we pass,
Bland, blessed Autumn! to our grave like thee,
Mid the green memories of unnumber'd hearts

TO-MORROW.

ONCE when the traveller's coach o'er England's vales
Paused at its destined goal, an aged crone
Came from a neighbouring cottage, with such speed
As weary years might make, and with red eye
Scanning each passenger, in hurried tones
Demanded, "*Has he come?*"

"No, not to-day;
To-morrow," was the answer. So, she turn'd,
Raising her shrivel'd finger, with a look
Half-credulous, half-reproachful, murmuring low,
"*To-morrow*," and went homeward.

A sad tale
Was hers, they said. She and her husband shared,
From early days, a life of honest toil,
Content, though poor. One only son they had,
Healthful and bright, and to their simple thought
Both wise and fair. The father was a man
Austere and passionate, who loved his boy
With pride that could not bear to brook his faults

Nor patiently to mend them. As he grew
Toward man's estate, the mother's readier tact
Discern'd the change of character that meets
With chafing neck the yoke of discipline,
And humour'd it; while to the sire he seem'd
Still but a child, and so he treated him.
When eighteen summers threw a ripening tinge
O'er brow and cheek, the father, at some fault
Born more of rashness than of turpitude,
Struck him in wrath, and turn'd him from his door
With bitter words. The youth, who shared too deep
The fiery temper of his father's blood,
Vow'd to return no more.

The mother wept,
And wildly pray'd her husband to forgive,
And call him back. But he, with aspect stern,
Bade her be silent, adding that the boy
Was by her folly and indulgence spoil'd
Beyond reclaim. And so she shuddering took
The tear and prayer back to her inmost soul,
And waited till the passion-storm should slack,
And die away. Long was that night of wo,
Yet mid its dreary watch, she thank'd her God
When, after hours of tossing, blessed sleep
Stole o'er the moody man. With quiet morn
Relentings came, and that ill-smother'd pang

With which an unruled spirit takes the lash
Of keen remorse. Awhile with shame he strove,
And then he bade the woman seek her son,
If so she will'd. Alas! it was too late.
He was a listed soldier for a land
Beyond the seas, nor would their little all
Suffice to buy him back.

'Twere long to tell
How pain and loneliness and sorrow took
Their Shylock-payment for that passion-gust.
Or how the father, when his hour had come,
Said, with a trembling lip and hollow voice,
"Would that our boy were here!" or how the wife,
In tenderest ministrations round his bed,
And in her widow'd mourning, echoed still
His dying words, "Oh! that our boy were here."

Years sped, and oft her soldier's letters came
Replete with filial love, and penitence,
And promise of return. But then, her soul
Was wrung by cruel tidings, that he lay
Wounded and sick in foreign hospitals.
A line traced faintly by his own dear hand
Relieved the torture. He was order'd home,
Among the invalids.

Joy, long unknown

Rush'd through her desolate heart. To hear his voice,
To gaze into his eyes, to part the locks
On his pure forehead, to prepare his food,
And nurse his feebleness, she ask'd no more.

Again his childhood's long forsaken couch
Put forth its snowy pillow, and once more,
The well-saved curtain of flower'd muslin deck'd
The lowly casement where he erst did love
To sit and read.
The cushion'd chair, that cheer'd
His father's lingering sickness, should be his;
And on the little table at his side
The hour-glass stood, whose ever-shifting sands
Had pleased him when a boy.
The appointed morn
Drew slowly on. The cheerful coals were heap'd
In the small grate, and ere the coach arrived
She with her throbbing heart stood eager there.
"Has Willie come?"
Each traveller, intent
On his own destination, heeded not
To make reply. "Coachman! is Willie there?"

"Willie? No! no!" in a hoarse, hurried voice,
Came the gruff answer. "Know ye not he's dead,

Good woman? *Dead!* And buried on the coast,
Four days ago."

But a kind stranger mark'd
How the strong surge of speechless agony
Swept o'er each feature, and in pity said,
"*Perchance he'll come to-morrow.*"

Home she went,
Struck to the soul, and wept the livelong night,
Insensible to comfort, and to all
Who spake the usual words of sympathy,
Answering nothing.

But when day return'd,
And the slight hammer of the cottage-clock
Announced the hour at which her absent son
Had been expected, suddenly she rose,
And dress'd herself and threw her mantle on,
And as the coachman check'd his foaming steeds,
Stood eager by his side. "Is Willie there?
My Willie? Say!"

While he, by pity school'd,
Answer'd, "*To-morrow.*"

And though years have fled,
And still her limbs grow weaker, and the hairs
Whiter and thinner on her wrinkled brow,
Yet duly, when the shrill horn o'er the hills
Preludeth the approaching traveller

That poor, demented woman hurries forth
To speak her only question, and receive
That one reply, *To-morrow.*
And on that
Fragment of hope deferr'd, doth her worn heart
Feed and survive. Lull'd by those syren words,
"*To-morrow*," which from childhood's trustful dawn
Have lured us all. When Reason sank
In the wild wreck of Grief, maternal Love
Caught at that empty sound, and clasp'd it close,
And grappled to it, like a broken oar,
To breast the shoreless ocean of despair.

EVE.

For the first time, a lovely scene
Earth saw, and smiled,—
A gentle form with pallid mien
Bending o'er a new-born child:
The pang, the anguish, and the wo
That speech hath never told,
Fled, as the sun with noontide glow
Dissolves the snow-wreath cold,
Leaving the bliss that none but mothers know;
While he, the partner of her heaven-taught joy,
Knelt in adoring praise beside his beauteous boy.

She, first of all our mortal race,
Learn'd the ecstasy to trace
The expanding form of infant grace
From her own life-spring fed;
To mark, each radiant hour,
Heaven's sculpture still more perfect growing,
More full of power;

The little foot's elastic tread,
The rounded cheek, like rose-bud glowing,
The fringed eye with gladness flowing,
As the pure, blue fountains roll;
And then those lisping sounds to hear,
Unfolding to her thrilling ear
The strange, mysterious, never-dying soul,
And with delight intense
To watch the angel-smile of sleeping innocence.

No more she mourn'd lost Eden's joy,
Or wept her cherish'd flowers,
In their primeval bowers
By wrecking tempests riven;
The thorn and thistle of the exile's lot
She heeded not,
So all-absorbing was her sweet employ
To rear the incipient man,* the gift her God had given.

And when his boyhood bold
A richer beauty caught,
Her kindling glance of pleasure told
The incense of her idol-thought:

* "I have gotten a man from the Lord." GEN. iv. 1.

Not for the born of clay
Is pride's exulting thrill,
Dark herald of the downward way,
And ominous of ill.
Even his cradled brother's smile
The haughty first-born jealously survey'd,
And envy mark'd the brow with hate and guile,
In God's own image made.

At the still twilight hour,
When saddest images have power,
Musing Eve her fears exprest:—
"He loves me not; no more with fondness free
His clear eye looks on me;
Dark passions rankle there, and moody hate
Predicts some adverse fate.
Ah! is this he, whose waking eye,
Whose faint, imploring cry,
With new and unimagined rapture blest?
Alas! alas! the throes his life that bought,
Were naught to this wild agony of thought
That racks my boding breast."

So mourn'd our mother, in her secret heart,
With presage all too true;

And often from the midnight dream would start,
Her forehead bathed in dew;
But say, what harp shall dare,
Unless by hand immortal strung,
What pencil touch the hue,
Of that intense despair
Her inmost soul that wrung!
For Cain was wroth, and in the pastures green,
Where Abel led his flock, mid waters cool and sheen,
With fratricidal hand, that blameless shepherd slew.

Earth learn'd strong lessons in her morning prime,
More strange than Chaos taught,
When o'er contending elements the darkest veil was wrought;
The poison of the tempter's glozing tongue,
Man's disobedience and expulsion dire,
The terror of the sword of fire
At Eden's portal hung,
Inferior creatures filled with savage hate,
No more at peace, no more subordinate;
Man's birth in agony, man's death by crime,
The taste of life-blood, brother-spilt;
But that red stain of guilt
Sent through her inmost heart such sickening pain,
That in her path o'er ether's plain
She hid her head and mourn'd, amid the planet-train.

BELL OF THE WRECK.

The bell of the steamer Atlantic, lost in Long-Island Sound, Nov. 25th, 1846, being supported by portions of the wreck and the contiguous rock, continued to toll, swept by wind and surge, the requiem of the dead.

Toll, toll, toll,
  Thou bell by billows swung,
And night and day thy warning words
  Repeat with mournful tongue!
Toll for the queenly boat,
  Wreck'd on yon rocky shore;
Sea-weed is in her palace-halls,
  She rides the surge no more!

Toll for the master bold,
  The high-soul'd and the brave,
Who ruled her like a thing of life
  Amid the crested wave!
Toll for the hardy crew,
  Sons of the storm and blast,
Who long the tyrant Ocean dared,
  But it vanquish'd them at last!

Toll for the man of God,
  Whose hallow'd voice of prayer
Rose calm above the stifled groan
  Of that intense despair!
How precious were those tones
  On that sad verge of life,
Amid the fierce and freezing storm,
  And the mountain-billows' strife!

Toll for the lover lost
  To the summon'd bridal train!
Bright glows a picture on his breast,
  Beneath the unfathom'd main.
One from her casement gazeth
  Long o'er the misty sea;
He cometh not, pale maiden,
  His heart is cold to thee!

Toll for the absent sire,
  Who to his home drew near,
To bless a glad expecting group,
  Fond wife, and children dear!
They heap the blazing hearth,
  The festal board is spread,
But a fearful guest is at the gate:
  Room for the sheeted dead!

Toll for the loved and fair,
The whelm'd beneath the tide,
The broken harps around whose strings
The dull sea-monsters glide!
Mother and nursling sweet,
Reft from the household throng;
There's bitter weeping in the nest
Where breath'd their soul of song.

Toll for the hearts that bleed
'Neath misery's furrowing trace!
Toll for the hapless orphan left
The last of all his race!
Yea, with thy heaviest knell
From surge to rocky shore,
Toll for the living, not the dead,
Whose mortal woes are o'er!

Toll, toll, toll,
O'er breeze and billow free,
And with thy startling lore instruct
Each rover of the sea;
Tell how o'er proudest joys
May swift destruction sweep,
And bid him build his hopes on high,
Lone Teacher of the deep!

WINTER AND AGE.

GRAY Winter loveth silence. He is old,
And liketh not the sporting of the lambs,
Nor the shrill song of birds. It irketh him
To hear the forest melodies, though still
He giveth license to the ruffian winds,
That, with black foreheads and distended cheeks,
Mutter hoarse thunders on their wrecking path.

He lays his finger on the lip of streams,
And they are ice; and stays the merry foot
Of the slight runlet, as it leapeth down,
Terrace by terrace, from the mountain's head.
He silenceth the purling of the brook,
That told its tale in gentle summer's ear
All the day long reproachless, and doth bid
Sharp frosts chastise and chain it, till it shrink
Abash'd away.
He sits with wrinkled face,
Like some old grandsire, ill at ease, who shuts

The noisy trooping of the children out,
And drawing nearer to the pleasant fire,
Doth settle on his head the velvet cap,
And bless his stars for quiet once again.
Stern winter drives the truant fountain back
To the dark caverns of the imprisoning earth,
And deadeneth with his drifted snows the sound
Of wheel and foot-tramp.
Thus it is with man,
When the chill winter of his life draws on.
The ear doth loathe the sounds that erst it loved,
Or, like some moody hermit, bar the door,
Though sweetest tones solicit it in vain.
The eye grows weary of the tarnish'd scenes
And old wind-shaken tapestries of time,
While all the languid senses antedate
The Sabbath of the tomb.
The echoing round
Of giddy pleasures, where his heart in youth
Disported eagerly, the rushing tread
Of the great, gorgeous world, are nought to him,
Who, as he journeyeth to a clime unknown,
Would to the skirts of holy silence cling,
And let all sounds and symphonies of earth
Fall like a faded vestment from the soul.

BIRDS OF PASSAGE.

NOVEMBER came on, with an eye severe,
And his stormy language was hoarse to hear,
And the glittering garland of gold and red,
Which was wreath'd for a while round the forest's head,
With sudden anger he rent away,
And all was cheerless and bare and gray.

Then the houseless grasshopper told his woes,
And the humming-bird sent forth a wail for the rose,
And the spider, that weaver of cunning so deep,
Roll'd himself up in a ball to sleep;
And the cricket his merry horn laid by
On the shelf, with the pipe of the dragon-fly.

Soon the birds were heard, at the morning prime,
Consulting of flight to a warmer clime:
"Let us go! let us go!" said the bright-wing'd jay;
And his gay spouse sang from a rocking spray,

"I am tired to death of this humdrum tree;
I'll go, if 'tis only the world to see!"

"Will you go?" ask'd the robin, "my only love?"
And a tender strain from the leafless grove
Responded, "Wherever your lot is cast,
Mid summer skies or the northern blast,
I am still at your side all your wanderings to cheer,
Though dear is our nest in the thicket here."

"I am ready to go," cried the querulous wren,
"From the wind-swept homes of these northern men;
My throat is sore, and my feet are blue;
I fear I have caught the consumption too."
And the oriole told, with a flashing eye,
How his plumage was dimm'd by this frosty sky.

Then up went the thrush with a trumpet call,
And the martins came forth from their cells on the wall,
And the owlets peep'd out from their secret bower,
And the swallows conversed on the old church-tower,
And the council of blackbirds was long and loud,
Chattering and flying from tree to cloud.

"The dahlia is dead on her throne," said they,
"And we saw the butterfly cold as clay;

Not a berry is found on the russet plains,
Not a kernel of ripen'd maize remains;
Every worm is hid—shall we longer stay
To be wasted with famine? Away! away!"

But what a strange clamour on elm and oak
From a bevy of brown-coated mocking-birds broke;
The theme of each separate speaker they told,
In a shrill report, with such mimicry bold,
That the eloquent orators started to hear
Their own true echo, so wild and clear.

Then tribe after tribe, with its leader fair,
Swept off through the fathomless depths of air.
Who marketh their course to the tropics bright?
Who nerveth their wing for its weary flight?
Who guideth that caravan's trackless way,
By the star at night and the cloud by day?

Some spread o'er the waters a daring wing,
In the isles of the southern sea to sing,
Or where the minaret, towering high,
Pierces the blue of the Moslem sky,
Or mid the harem's haunts of fear,
Their lodgings to build, and their nurslings rear.

The Indian fig, with its arching screen,
Welcomes them in to its vistas green,
And the breathing buds of the spicy tree
Thrill at the burst of their melody,
And the bulbul starts, mid his carol clear,
Such a rushing of stranger-wings to hear.

Oh wild wood-wanderers! how far away
From your rural homes in our vales ye stray;
But when they are waked by the touch of Spring,
Shall we see you again with your glancing wing,
Your nests mid our household trees to raise,
And fill our hearts with our Maker's praise?

AARON ON MOUNT HOR.

THE summer-day declined o'er Edom's vales,
As on, through rugged paths of lone Mount Hor,
Three men went travelling slow.
One, whose white beard
O'erswept his reverend breast, moved painful on,
And ever, as the ascent steeper grew,
More wearily did lean on those who lent
Their kindly aid.
I see the mitred brow
Of the High Priest of Israel, and anon,
As the slant sun sends forth some brighter beam
Through the sparse boughs and cones of terebinth,
His dazzling breastplate like a rainbow gleams.

He muses o'er the distant Past, and calls
The buried years. Each, like unwilling ghost,
Comes up with its dark scroll and glides away.
Again the moan of Egypt meets his ear,
As when her first-born died; the sounding surge

Of the divided sea, enforced to leave
Its ancient channels; the affrighted cry
Of Israel at red Sinai's awful base;
Their murmurings and their mockings and their strife;
The sin at Meribah; the desert-graves
Fed with a rebel race,—all rise anew,
And, like the imagery of troubled dreams,
Enwrap the spirit.
With what earnest eye
And mournful, from the topmost cliff he gazed.
There, stretching round its base, like sprinkled snow
Were Israel's tents, where lay in brief repose
The desert-wearied tribes.
Through distant haze
Gleam'd Edom's roofs, with shadowy palm-trees blent;
While farther still, like a black Stygian pool,
The lone Dead Sea its sullen waters roll'd.

He turn'd, and lo! Mount Seir with frowning brow
Confronted him. All solemn and severe
Was its uncover'd forehead. Did it rise
Like witness stern, to stir with vengeful hand
The sleeping memories of forgotten things,
That probe the conscience?
Once again he bent
To mark the tents of Jacob. Fair they seem'd,

Amid lign-aloes and the cedars tall
That God had planted;—fairer than to him,
That recreant prophet, who was yet to spy
The chosen people, resting on their way,
And by fierce Balak's side, from Peor's top
Take up his parable, changing the curse
Into a blessing.
But to Aaron's eye,
The haunts his feet must ne'er revisit more
Put on new beauty. For the parting hour
Unveils the love that like a stranger hides
In the heart's depths.
Was that his own sweet home,
Its curtains floating, as the southern breeze
Woo'd its white folds?
He pass'd his arm around
His brother's shoulder, leaning heavily,
And lower o'er his bosom droop'd his head,
In that long, farewell look, which by no sound
Reveal'd its import to the mortal ear.

Anon his features wear a brightening tinge,
And o'er his high anointed brow breaks forth
A gleam of joy. Caught he a glorious view
Of that eternal Canaan, fair with light,

And water'd by the river of his God,
Where was his heritage?

Or stole a strain
From Miriam's timbrel, o'er the flood of death
Urging him onward, through the last faint steps
Of toil-worn life?

And now they reach the spot
Where he had come to die. Strange heaviness
Settled around his spirit. Then he knew
That death's dark angel stretch'd a sable wing
'Tween him and earth. The altar, and the ark,
The unutter'd mysteries seen within the vail,
Those deep-set traces of his inmost soul,
Grew dim and vanish'd.

So, with trembling hand,
He hasted to unclasp the priestly robe
And cast it o'er his son, and on his head
The mitre place; while, with a feeble voice,
He bless'd, and bade him keep his garments pure
From blood of souls. But then, as Moses raised
The mystic breastplate, and that dying eye
Caught the last radiance of those precious stones,
By whose oracular and fearful light
Jehovah had so oft his will reveal'd
Unto the chosen tribes, whom Aaron loved,
In all their wanderings—but whose promised land

He might not look upon—he sadly laid
His head upon the mountain's turfy breast,
And with one prayer, half wrapp'd in stifled groans,
Gave up the ghost.
Steadfast beside the dead,
With folded arms and face uplift to heaven
The prophet Moses stood, as if by faith
Following the sainted soul. No sigh of grief
Nor sign of earthly passion mark'd the man
Who once on Sinai's top had talked with God.
—But the young priest knelt down, with quivering lip,
And press'd his forehead on the pulseless breast,
And, mid the gifts of sacerdotal power
And dignity intrusted to his hand,
Remembering but the father that he loved,
Long with his filial tears bedew'd the clay.

ADVERTISEMENT OF A LOST DAY.

Lost! lost! lost!
  A gem of countless price,
Cut from the living rock,
  And graved in Paradise;
Set round with three times eight
  Large diamonds, clear and bright,
And each with sixty smaller ones,
  All changeful as the light.

Lost—where the thoughtless throng
  In fashion's mazes wind,
Where trilleth folly's song,
  Leaving a sting behind;
Yet to my hand 'twas given
  A golden harp to buy,
Such as the white-robed choir attune
  To deathless minstrelsy.

Lost! lost! lost!
  I feel all search is vain;
That gem of countless cost
  Can ne'er be mine again;
I offer no reward,
  For till these heart-strings sever,
I know that Heaven-intrusted gift
  Is reft away for ever.

But when the sea and land
  Like burning scroll have fled,
I'll see it in His hand
  Who judgeth quick and dead;
And when of scath and loss
  That man can ne'er repair,
The dread inquiry meets my soul,
  What shall it answer there?

STORM-SAILS.

Out with thy storm-sails, for the blast is loud,
And seas and skies commingle.
Pleasant smiles,
Fond cheering hopes, delightful sympathies,
Story and song, the needle's varied skill,
The shaded lamp, the glowing grate at eve,
The page made vocal by a taste refined,
Imparted memories, plans for others' good,
These are a woman's storm-sails. Fain we'd keep
Each one in readiness, whene'er the cloud
Maketh our home our fortress, and debars
Egress abroad.
So, choose ye which to spread,
My fair young lady. For the foot of youth
Is nimblest mid the shrouds of social life,
And readiest should its fairy hand unfurl
The household banner of true happiness.
What has thy brow to do with frowns? thy heart
With selfish lore? as yet, so little school'd

In the world's venal traffic. Make thine eye
A cheering light-house to the voyager
Wearied and worn. Shed blessed hope on all,
Parent, fraternal group, or transient guest;
Nor let the toiling servant be forgot,
Who in the casket of remembrance stores
Each word of praise.
Mother, when tempests rage,
Draw thy young children nearer. Let them share
The intercourse that, while it soothes, instructs,
And elevates the soul. Implant some germ
Of truth, or tenderness, or holy faith,
And trust the rain of heaven to water it.
So shall those sweet, unfolding blossoms blend
In future years thine image with the storm,
Like the pure rainbow, with its glorious scroll
Teaching of God.
Scholar, and child of rhyme,
This is thy holiday. No vexing fear
Of interruption, and no idler's foot
Shall mar thy revery.
And while the flame
Of blissful impulse nerves thy flying pen,
Write on thy storm-sails deathless thoughts to guide
Thy wind-swept brother to the port of peace.

THE SCOTTISH WEAVER.

As hasting night o'er Scotia's plains
  Its murky mantle flung,
And on its skirts with ruffian wrath
  A threatening tempest hung,

Beside a farm-house door, a voice
  Rose o'er the howling blast,
"Ah! give us shelter from the storm,
  The darkness gathers fast.

"We are not vagrants, God forbid!
  A dark and evil day,
That made so many looms stand still,
  Hath taken our bread away.

"And now, to Inverary's vales,
  In search of work we go,
And thrice the setting sun hath seen
  Our way-worn course, and slow.

"My wife a nursing infant bears,
Three younglings at her side,
Weary and cold,"—but churlish tones
The earnest suit denied.

"The humblest shed is all we ask,
Your food we will not crave,
And blessings on your head shall rest
E'en till we find a grave.

"Ah! for our dear Redeemer's sake,
Let us till morning stay,"
The harsh key grated in its ward,—
The suppliant turn'd away.

He held his hand before his face
To bar the blinding sleet,
And sorrow'd for those hearts that soon
Such dread repulse must meet.

"O husband, you have linger'd long;
'Tis lonesome on the wold;
Up, bairnies, to yon bonny house,
And shield ye from the cold."

The wretched man bent shuddering down,
 Scarce kenn'd he what to say,
He could not find it in his heart
 To take her hope away.

Yet o'er the moor, for many a league,
 All desolate and drear,
He knew no other dwelling rose,
 The traveller's sight to cheer.

"Jeanie, my poor and patient wife,
 God give thee strength to bear;
'Neath yonder roof we may not bide,
 There is no mercy there."

The weary woman groan'd aloud:
 "Not for myself I cry,
But for the babe that feebly pines,
 Methinks its death is nigh."

The little children sobb'd and wept,
 And, clinging round her, said,
"O mother! mother! 'tis *so* long
 Since you have given us bread."

The pitying father hush'd their grief,
  And drew them to his side,
Till sleep, the angel, on their cheeks
  The trickling sorrow dried;

Then spread his mantle o'er their breasts,
  Scant though it was and poor,
And there mid driving snows they cower'd,
  Upon the dreary moor.

Wild throbb'd his aching head, and wide
  His starting eyeballs strain,
While through the darkness, lurid fires
  Seem'd flashing from his brain:

Strange phantom-forms went gibbering by,
  And woke to fearful strife
The thoughts that nerve the reckless hand
  Against the traveller's life.

A new and dauntless strength he felt,
  Like giant in his prime,
Such strength as drives the madden'd wretch
  To judgment ere his time.

But from the fountain of his soul
Uprose a contrite prayer,
That Heaven would crush the seeds of crime,
And break the tempter's snare.

Kind tones the awful revery broke,
A human form drew near,
An humble serving-man who mark'd
Their misery severe;

One who the stern denial heard
That check'd the plaint of need,
And ventured to an outhouse rude
The hapless group to lead.

Oh poor man, who thyself hast quaked
'Neath hunger-pang, and cold,
Or felt the lashing of the winds
Through garments thin and old;

Far better canst thou feel for those
Who bide misfortune's blast,
Than Plenty's proud and pamper'd sons
Who share the rich repast,

Who, lapp'd in luxury, rejoice
  By fireside bright and warm,
Or from their curtain'd pillow list
  The howling of the storm.

Rest to those wearied ones, how sweet!
  E'en on that pauper-bed,
The tatter'd blanket o'er them cast,
  The straw beneath them spread.

But, at gray dawn, a piercing shriek!
  Hark to that wild despair!
"My babe! my babe! she breathes no more!"
  Oh Spoiler! art thou there?

That ghastly face the children mark'd
  As up from sleep they sprang,
The thin blue fingers clench'd so close
  In the last hunger-pang.

And pitiful it was to see
  How meagre want and care
Had set the wasting seal of years
  On brow so small and fair.

Loud rose the wail of childhood's wo:
"Will she not wake again,
Our play-mate sister? Never more?"
Keen was that transient pain.

But whosoe'er hath chanced to hear
A mother's cry of dread,
Who, waking, on her bosom finds
Her nursling cold and dead,—

Its nerveless lip empower'd no more
The fount of life to press,
And gleeful smile and speaking eye
Mute to the fond caress,—

I say, whoe'er that sound hath heard
Invade his lone retreat,
Will keep the echo in his soul
While memory holds her seat.

The father started to her side,
He spoke no word of wo;
Words!—would they dare in such an hour
Their poverty to show?

E'en manly nature reel'd to meet
  Such sudden shock of grief,—
And drowning thought to trifles clung,
  In search of vain relief.

The swallows, startled from their nests
  By pain's discordant sound,
Among the rafters bare and brown
  Went circling round and round;

And gazing on their aimless flight,
  He strove, with futile care,
To parry for a little space
  The anguish of despair.

But now, e'en hardest human hearts
  With sympathy were fraught,
For late remorse the kindness woke
  That pity should have taught.

There lay the babe so still and cold,
  Crush'd 'neath affliction's weight,
For whom, perchance, their earlier care
  Had won a longer date;

But in the churchyard's grassy bound
  A narrow spot they gave,
With tardy charity, that yields—
  Instead of bread—*a grave.*

Sad tears of agonizing grief
  Bedew'd the darling's clay,
And then that stricken-hearted group
  Pursued their mournful way.

O'er Scotia's glens and mountains rude
  A toilsome path they wound,
Or 'neath some cotter's lowly roof
  A nightly shelter found,

Until, mid Inverary's vales,
  Once more a home they knew,
And from the father's earnest hand
  The unresting shuttle flew.

And though but scant the dole he earn'd,
  Yet prudence found a way
To make it satisfy the needs
  Of each returning day.

So, to her parents' heavy lot
  Some filial aid to lend,
The eldest, Bessie, left her home,
  A shepherd's flock to tend.

Unceasing, for her helpless ones,
  The industrious mother strove,
And season'd still the homeliest meal
  With sweet maternal love.

Oft, when the quiet gloaming fell
  O'er heathery field and hill,
And 'tween the daylight and the dark
  Her busier toils were still,

She told them wild and stirring tales
  Of Scotia's old renown,
And of the Bruce who bravely won,
  In evil times, the crown;

Or sang, to rouse their patriot zeal,
  Some high, heroic stave;
Or whisper'd, through her swelling tears,
  Of their lost sister's grave;

Or bade them duly, night and morn,
Whene'er they knelt in prayer,
To supplicate for Bessie dear
Their God's protecting care.

Yet joyous was the hour when they,
With shout and gambol fleet,
Went bounding from the cottage door
The approaching sire to greet,

Who twice a month, from distant scenes
Of weary toil and care,
Walk'd three times three long Scottish miles
To spend his Sabbath there.

And when, like lone and glimmering star,
Across the heath he spied
The rush-light in the window placed
His homeward steps to guide,

Methought a spirit's wing was his,
From all obstruction free,
Till by his Jeanie's side he sate,
The wee things on his knee.

There, while the humble fire of peat
  A flickering radiance threw,
The oatmeal parritch had a zest
  The unloving never knew.

And from the poor man's thrilling heart
  Such grateful praise arose,
As they have never learn'd to breathe
  Who never shared his woes.

Once, when the hallow'd day of rest
  Had pass'd serenely by,
And evening with its sober vail
  Encompass'd earth and sky,

Their cottage worship duly paid,
  While from the pallet near,
The little sleepers' breathing fell
  Like music on their ear,

The faithful pair with kind discourse
  Beguiled the gathering shade,
As fitful o'er the darken'd wall
  The blinking ingle play'd.

Then Jeanie many a soothing word
 To Willie's heart address'd,
Her head upon his shoulder laid,
 His arm around her press'd.

Much of their bairnies' weal she spake,
 And with confiding air
Incited for their tender years
 A father's watchful care,

With tearful eye and trembling tone,
 As one about to trust
Fond treasures to another's hand,
 And slumber in the dust.

Her heavenly hopes, she said, were bright,
 But mortal life was frail,
And something, whispering, warn'd her soul
 That soon her strength might fail.

"Oh, Willie dearest! ne'er before
 I've stay'd thy lingering tread,
For well I know 'tis hard to take
 The time that earns our bread.

"But now one single day I ask,
  For then, the weight that bow'd
My spirit with its presage dire,
  May prove an April cloud."

He stay'd, to mark the fearful pang
  That hath not yet been told,
To see the livid hues of death
  The rigid brow unfold.

He stay'd, to find all help was vain,
  Ere the next evening-tide,
And then to lay her in the grave,
  Her new-born babe beside.

Her new-born babe! With her it died,
  And in the white shroud's fold,
Fast by her marble breast 'twas seen,
  A blossom crush'd and cold.

Oh wounded and forsaken man!
  Whom mocking Hope doth flee,
The lingering luxury of grief
  Is not for such as thee.

Stern Toil doth summon thee away,
And thou the call must hear,
As the lone Arab strikes his tent
To roam the desert drear.

He closed the pleasant room where late
His cheerful hearth had burn'd,
And to the waiting landlord's hand
The household key return'd.

And to a pitying neighbour's door
His youngest nursling led,
Too weak to try the weary road
It was his lot to tread,—

With earnest words bespoke her care,
Which he would well repay,
Then bless'd the poor, unconscious boy,
And sadly turn'd away.

With wondering eyes, the stranger-child
The unwonted scene survey'd,
And to the darkest corner shrank,
Bewilder'd and afraid.

From thence, escaping to his home
  With bosom swelling high,
Uplifted, as he fled away,
  A loud and bitter cry;

And wildly call'd his mother's name,
  And press'd the unyielding door,
And breathless listen'd for the voice
  That he must hear no more.

And, then, the holy hymn she taught
  He lisp'd with simple wile,
As if that talisman were sure
  To win her favouring smile.

But when all efforts fruitless proved,
  Exhausted with his moan,
The orphan sobb'd himself to sleep
  Upon the threshold-stone.

Even passing travellers paused to mark
  A boy, so young and fair,
Thus slumbering on a stony bed
  Amid the nipping air,—

A boy, whose flaxen curls, the care
Of matron love disclose,
Though sorrow's pearl-drops sprinkled lay
Upon his cheeks of rose.

But onward, toward his lot of toil
With spirit bow'd and bent,
Wee Willie walking by his side,
The widow'd father went.

Silent they journey'd, hand in hand,
While from its cloud-wrapp'd head
A shower of chill and drizzling mist
The bleak Benachie shed.

Then, from the beaten track they turn'd
A broken path to wind,
The lonely spot where Bessie dwelt,
In a far glen to find.

They wander'd long o'er strath and brae,
While blasts autumnal sweep,
Before their own poor girl they spied
Tending her snowy sheep.

Up toward the mountain side she gazed,
  Intent, yet sad of cheer,
Expecting still, from hour to hour,
  To greet her mother dear.

Alas! this was the appointed day
  On which that tender friend
Had promised with her loving child
  A little time to spend.

Warm stockings, that her hand would knit
  From fleecy wool, to bring;
Perchance, a broader plaid, to shield
  From coming winter's sting.

As bounds the glad and nimble deer,
  She flew, their steps to meet;
"Father! and Willie! welcome here!
  But where's my mother sweet?"

"Speak to her, Willie! Kiss her cheek!
  That grows so pale and white;
Fain would I turn away awhile,
  I cannot bear the sight.

"O sob not so, my precious son!
Speak kindly words, and say
Why your lost mother does not come,
And how she sleeps in clay."

So, clasp'd within each other's arms,
Upon the heather dry,
Beside a clear and rippling brook
That crept unheeded by,

They told their tale of wo, and found
In sympathy relief;
But he, the deeper mourner, sank,
In solitary grief.

And nought escaped his utterance there,
While kneeling on the sod,
Save her loved name, his poor lost wife,
And broken cries to God.

Nor long the kindred tear to pour
That smitten group might stay,
For meagre Want with tyrant frown
Were beckoning them away.

"Oh, put your trust in God, my child,"
The parting father said,
Then kiss'd his daughter's trembling lips,
And on his journey sped.

And sometimes, when her task bore hard,
It seem'd a mother's sigh,
"Oh, put your trust in God, my child,"
Came breathing from the sky.

Oh ye, who see the suffering poor
With countless ills opprest,
Yet on in lordly chariots roll,
Nor heed their sad request;—

Who mark the unrequited toil
That with its mountain weight
Doth crush them hopeless to the dust,
Yet leave them to their fate;

Think of the hour, when forth, like theirs,
Your uncloth'd soul must fleet,
Its last and dread account to bide
Before the Judge's seat.

And if to feed the hungering poor,
And be the orphan's stay,
Shall be remember'd mid the ire
Of that terrific day,

Haste! ope the hand to mercy's deed,
The heart to sorrow's prayer,
And bid your lowly brother plead
For your forgiveness there.

NOTE.

"Strange to say, on first becoming aware of the bereavements of that terrible night, I sate for some minutes gazing upward at the fluttering and wheeling movements of a party of swallows, our fellow-lodgers, that had been disturbed by our unearthly outcry."—*Recollections of a Hand-loom Weaver.*

This poem is almost a literal version of circumstances related in a book, with the above title, published in England recently, and written by William Thom, a Scotch weaver and poet. "Its object," says the author, "is to impart to one portion of the community glimpses of what is going on in another."

In our own happy land, the labouring poor have no idea of the distress which he thus simply yet forcibly depicts. It occurred soon after six thousand looms were stopped in the region of Dundee, and just before William Thom, with his wife and four little ones, left their home at Newlyte, in search of the means of subsistence at Inverary, as related in the preceding stanzas.

"It had been a stiff winter and an unkindly spring; but I will not expatiate on six human lives maintained on five shillings weekly, on babies prematurely thoughtful, on comely faces withering, on desponding youth, and too quickly declining age. I will describe one morning of modified starvation at Newlyte, and then pass on.

"Imagine a cold, dreary forenoon. It is eleven o'clock, but our little dwelling shows none of the signs of that time of day. The four children are still asleep. There is a bed-cover hung before the window, to keep all within as much like night as possible. The mother sits beside the bed of her children, to lull them back to sleep, when either shall show any inclination to wake. For this there is a cause. Our weekly five shillings have not come as was expected, and the only food in the house consists of a handful of oatmeal saved from the supper of last night. Our fuel is also exhausted. My wife and I were conversing in sunken whispers about making an attempt to cook the handful of meal, when the youngest child awoke, beyond the mother's power to hush it again to sleep. It finally broke out into a steady scream, which, of course, rendered it impossible to keep the rest in a state of unconsciousness. Face after face sprang up, each little one exclaiming, 'O mother! mother! give me a piece.' How weak a word is *sorrow*, to apply to the feelings of myself and my wife on that dreary day!"

THE INDIAN SUMMER.

WHEN was the red man's summer?
When the rose
Hung its first banner out? When the gray rock,
Or the brown heath, the radiant kalmia clothed?
Or when the loiterer by the reedy brooks
Started to see the proud lobelia glow
Like living flame? When through the forest gleam'd
The rhododendron? or the fragrant breath
Of the magnolia swept deliciously
O'er the half laden nerve?
No. When the groves
In fleeting colours wrote their own decay,
And leaves fell eddying on the sharpen'd blast
That sang their dirge; when o'er their rustling bed
The red deer sprang, or fled the shrill-voiced quail,
Heavy of wing and fearful; when, with heart
Foreboding or depress'd, the white man mark'd
The signs of coming winter: then began

The Indian's joyous season.* Then the haze,
Soft and illusive as a fairy dream,
Lapp'd all the landscape in its silvery fold.
The quiet rivers, that were wont to hide
'Neath shelving banks, beheld their course betray'd
By the white mist that o'er their foreheads crept,
While wrapp'd in morning dreams, the sea and sky
Slept 'neath one curtain, as if both were merged
In the same element. Slowly the sun,
And all reluctantly, the spell dissolved,
And then it took upon its parting wing
A rainbow glory.

Gorgeous was the time,
Yet brief as gorgeous. Beautiful to thee,
Our brother hunter, but to us replete
With musing thoughts in melancholy train.
Our joys, alas! too oft were wo to thee.
Yet ah, poor Indian! whom we fain would drive
Both from our hearts, and from thy father's lands,
The perfect year doth bear thee on its crown,
And when we would forget, repeat thy name.

---

* An aged chief said to our ancestors, "The white man's summer is past and gone, but that of the Indian begins when the leaves fall."

THE HERMIT OF THE FALLS.

It was the leafy month of June,
And joyous Nature, all in tune,
With wreathing buds was drest,
As toward Niagara's fearful side
A youthful stranger prest.
His ruddy cheek was blanch'd with awe,
And scarce he seem'd his breath to draw,
While, bending o'er its brim,
He mark'd its strong, unfathom'd tide,
And heard its thunder-hymn.

His measured week too quickly fled,
Another, and another sped,
And soon the summer rose decay'd,
The moon of autumn sank in shade,
Years fill'd their circle brief and fair,
Yet still the enthusiast linger'd there,

Till winter hurl'd its dart;
For deeply round his soul was wove
A mystic chain of quenchless love,
That would not let him part.
When darkest midnight veil'd the sky,
You'd hear his hasting step go by,
To gain the bridge beside the deep,
That thread-like o'er the surge
Shot, where the wildest torrents leap,
And there, upon its awful verge,
His vigil lone to keep.

And when the moon, descending low,
Hung on the flood that gleaming bow,
Which it would seem some angel's hand
With heaven's own pencil tinged and spann'd,
Pure symbol of a better land,
He, kneeling, poured in utterance free
The eloquence of ecstasy;
Though to his words no answer came,
Save that One, Everlasting Name,
Which, since Creation's morning broke,
Niagara's lip alone hath spoke.

When wintry tempests shook the sky,
And the rent pine-tree hurtled by,

Unblenching mid the storm he stood,
And mark'd sublime the wrathful flood,
While wrought the frost-king fierce and drear,
His palace mid those cliffs to rear,
And strike the massy buttress strong,
And pile his sleet the rocks among,
And wasteful deck the branches bare
With icy diamonds, rich and rare.

Nor lack'd the hermit's humble shed
  Such comforts as our natures ask
  To fit them for their daily task,—
The cheering fire, the peaceful bed,
The simple meal in season spread:
While by the lone lamp's trembling light,
As blazed the hearth-stone clear and bright,
  O'er Homer's page he hung,
Or Maro's martial numbers scann'd,
For classic lore of many a land
  Flow'd smoothly o'er his tongue.
Oft, with rapt eye and skill profound,
He woke the entrancing viol's sound,
  Or touch'd the sweet guitar,
For heavenly music deign'd to dwell
An inmate in his cloister'd cell,
  As beams the solemn star

All night, with meditative eyes,
Where some lone rock-bound fountain lies.
As through the groves with quiet tread,
On his accustom'd haunts he sped,
The mother-thrush, unstartled, sung
Her descant to her callow young,
And fearless o'er his threshold prest
The wanderer from the sparrow's nest;
The squirrel raised a sparkling eye,
Nor from his kernel cared to fly
As pass'd that gentle hermit by;
No timid creature shrank to meet
His pensive glance, serenely sweet;
From his own kind, alone, he sought
The screen of solitary thought.
Whether the world too harshly prest
Its iron o'er a yielding breast,
Or taught his morbid youth to prove
The pang of unrequited love,
We know not, for he never said
Aught of the life that erst he led.

On Iris isle, a summer bower
He twined with branch, and vine, and flower,
And there he mused, on rustic seat,
Unconscious of the noonday heat,

Or 'neath the crystal waters lay,
Luxuriant, in the swimmer's play.
Yet once, the whelming flood grew strong,
And bore him like a weed along,
Though, with convulsive throes of pain
And heaving breast, he strove in vain;
Then sinking 'neath the infuriate tide,
Lone as he lived, the hermit died.

On, by the rushing current swept,
The lifeless corse its voyage kept,
To where, in narrow gorge comprest,
The whirling eddies never rest,
But boil with wild tumultuous sway,
The maelstrom of Niagara.
And there, within that rocky bound,
In swift gyrations round and round,
Mysterious course it held;
Now springing from the torrent hoarse,
Now battling as with maniac force,
To mortal strife compell'd.

Right fearful 'neath the moonbeam bright,
It was to see that brow so white,
And mark the ghastly dead
Leap upward from his torture-bed,

As if in passion-gust,
And tossing wild with agony,
To mock the omnipotent decree
Of dust to dust.

At length, where smoother waters flow,
Emerging from the gulf below,
The hapless youth they gain'd, and bore
Sad to his own forsaken door.
There watch'd his dog with straining eye,
And scarce would let the train pass by,
Save that, with instinct's rushing spell,
Through the changed cheek's empurpled hue,
And stiff and stony form, he knew
The master he had loved so well.

The kitten fair, whose graceful wile
So oft had won his musing smile,
As at his foot she held her play,
Stretch'd on his vacant pillow lay.
While strew'd around, on board and chair,
The last pluck'd flower, the book last read,
The ready pen, the page outspread,
The water-cruse, the unbroken bread,
Reveal'd how sudden was the snare
That swept him to the dead.

And so he rests in foreign earth,
Who drew mid Albion's vales his birth;
Yet let no cynic phrase unkind
Condemn that youth of gentle mind,
Of shrinking nerve and lonely heart,
And letter'd lore and tuneful art,
Who here his humble worship paid,
In that most glorious temple-shrine,
Where to the Majesty divine
Nature her noblest altar made.

No, blame him not, but praise the Power
Who in the dear, domestic bower,
Hath given you firmer strength to rear
The plants of love with toil and fear,
The beam to meet, the blast to dare,
And like a faithful soldier bear.
Still with sad heart his requiem pour,
Amid the cataract's ceaseless roar,
Nor grudge one tear of pitying gloom
To dew that sad enthusiast's tomb.

ERIN'S DAUGHTER.

Poor Erin's daughter cross'd the main
  In youth's unfolding prime,
A lot of servitude to bear
  In this our western clime.

And when the drear heart-sickness came
  Beneath a stranger sky,
Tears on her nightly pillow lay,
  But morning saw them dry.

For still with earnest hope she strove
  Her distant home to cheer,
And from her parents lift the load
  Of poverty severe.

To them with liberal hand she sent
  Her all—her hard-earn'd store—
A rapture thrilling through her soul,
  She ne'er had felt before.

E'en mid her quiet slumbers gleam'd
  A cabin's lighted pane,
A board with simple plenty crown'd,
  A loved and loving train.

And so her life of earnest toil
  With secret joy was blest,
For the sweet warmth of filial love
  Made sunshine in her breast.

But bitter tidings o'er the wave
  With fearful echo sped;
Gaunt famine o'er her home had strode,
  And all were with the dead!

All gone!—her brothers in their glee,
  Her sisters young and fair;
And Erin's daughter bow'd her down
  In desolate despair.

THE HOLY DEAD.

"Wherefore I praised the dead who are already dead more than the living who are yet alive."—SOLOMON.

THEY dread no storm that lowers,
  No perish'd joys bewail;
They pluck no thorn-clad flowers,
  Nor drink of streams that fail:
There is no tear-drop in their eye,
  No change upon their brow;
Their placid bosom heaves no sigh
  Though all earth's idols bow.

Who are so greatly blest?
  From whom hath sorrow fled?
Who share such deep, unbroken rest
  Where all things toil? *The dead!*
The holy dead. Why weep ye so
  Above yon sable bier?
Thrice blessed! they have done with wo,
  The living claim the tear.

Go to their sleeping bowers,
  Deck their low couch of clay
With earliest spring's soft breathing flowers;
  And when they fade away,
Think of the amaranthine wreath,
  The garlands never dim,
And tell me why thou fly'st from death,
  Or hid'st thy friends from him.

We dream, but they awake;
  Dread visions mar our rest;
Through thorns and snares our way we take,
  And yet we mourn the blest!
For spirits round the Eternal Throne
  How vain the tears we shed!
They are the living, they alone,
  Whom thus we call *the dead.*

DEW-DROPS.

"FATHER, there are no dew-drops on my rose;
I thought to find them, but they all are gone.
Was night a niggard? Or did envious dawn
Steal those bright diamonds from unwaken'd day?"

The father answer'd not, but pointed where
The sudden falling of a summer shower
Made quiet music mid the quivering leaves,
And through the hollows of the freshen'd turf
Drew lines like silver. Then a bow sprang forth
Spanning the skies.
"See'st thou yon glorious hues,
Violet and gold? The dew-drops glitter there,
That from the bosom of thy rose had fled,
My precious child. Read thou their lesson well,
That what is pure and beautiful on earth
Shall smile in heaven."
He knew not that he spake

Prophetic words. But ere the infant moon
Swell'd to a perfect orb her crescent pale,
That loving soul, which on the parent's breast
Had sparkled as a dew-drop, was exhaled,
To mingle mid the brightness of the skies.

THE LITTLE FOOTSTEP.

I SAW a tiny footstep in the snow,
Beside a cottage door.
So slight it was,
And fairy-like, methought it scarce belong'd
To our terrestrial race. With zigzag course,
On the white element it left a trace,
While here and there, the likeness of a hand,
Each baby-finger like a spider's claw
Outspread to clutch, reveal'd some morsel cold,
Snatch'd, and by stealth to the red lip conveyed.
—Didst think 'twas sugar, child? and this round world
All one huge, frosted cake?
Others have made
Mistakes as strange, e'en though their locks were gray.

So musing on I went, until the track
Of that small creature was abruptly stay'd,
While trampling parallel, broad, heavy feet,

In backward lines, their giant impress made,
Quite to the cottage-gate.
Some pirate, sure,
Had captured the poor traveller, in the bud
And blossom of its joyous enterprise,
And, nolens volens, bore it home again.
Moreover, in the note-book of the snow
I read this capture was against its will,
For at the juncture of those differing feet,
Marks of a passion-struggle plainly told
A differing purpose; and I seem'd to hear
The angry shriek of the indignant child
Intent on freedom, and the smother'd wail
With which, at length, it yielded to the force
Of nurse or servant,—and to nursery drear,
Perchance to darken'd closet, for its fault
Was borne appall'd.
So, o'er the race of time,
Young fancy starts, unbridled, unarray'd,
Undisciplined, until stern Reason's grasp
Arrests the fugitive. Anon, the cares,
And toils, and tyrannies of time, dispel
Its frost-work fabrics. So, with pinion'd wing
And fallen crest, it yieldeth to their will,
Bearing "*sub jugum*" on its tattoo'd brow
Like some New Zealand chief.

A lesson strong,
Yet needful, thou hast in thy memory stored
This day, sad infant.

Liberty's excess
Is pruned within thee, and henceforth must know
Curb and restraint, till, like La Plata's steed,
It heed the lasso well.

Thus, may we gain,
We, older scholars in life's school austere,
From all its discipline a will subdued,
And, when its hour-glass closes, find at last
A Father's house, like thee.

SCOTLAND'S FAMINE.

THERE'S weeping mid the lonely sea
  Where the rude Hebrids lie,
And where the misty Highlands point
  Their foreheads to the sky.

The oats were blighted on the stalk,
  The corn before its bloom,
And many a hand that held the plough
  Is pulseless in the tomb.

There is no playing in the streets,
  The haggard children move
Like mournful phantoms, mute and slow,
  Uncheer'd by hope or love.

No dog upon his master fawns,
  No sheep the hillocks throng,
Not e'en the playmate kitten sports
  The sad-eyed babes among.

No more the cock his clarion sounds,
  Nor brooding wing is spread;
There is no food in barn or stall,
  The household birds are dead.

From the young maiden's hollow cheek
  The ruddy blush is gone,
The peasant like a statue stands,
  And hardens into stone.

The shuttle sleepeth in the loom,
  The crook upon the walls,
And from the languid mother's hand
  The long-used distaff falls.

She hears her children ask for bread,
  And what can she bestow?
She sees their uncomplaining sire
  A mournful shadow grow.

Oh Scotia! Sister! if thy woes
  Awake no pitying care,
If long at banquet-board we sit
  Nor heed thy deep despair,—

While thou art pining unto death,
  Amid thy heather brown,
Wilt not the Giver of our joys
  Upon our luxuries frown?

And blast the blossom of our pride,
  And ban the rusted gold,
And turn the morsel into gall
  That we from thee withhold?

FALLS OF THE YANTIC.

Hills, rocks, and waters! here ye lie,
And o'er ye spreads the same blue sky,
As when, in early days,
My childish foot your cliffs essay'd,
My wondering eye your depth survey'd,
Where the vex'd torrent stays.

O'er bolder scenes mine age hath stray'd
By floods that make your light cascade
Seem as an infant's play;
Yet dearer is it still to me,
Than all their boasted pageantry
That charms the traveller's way.

For here, enchanted, side by side,
With me would many a playmate glid
When school-day's task was o'er,
Who deem'd this world, from zone to zone,
Had nought of power or wonder known
Like thy resounding shore.

Light-hearted group! I see ye still,
For Memory's pencil, at her will,
    Doth tint ye bright and rare;
Red lips, from whence glad laughter rang,
Elastic limbs that tireless sprang,
    And curls of sunny hair.

I will not ask if change or care
Have coldly marr'd those features fair;
    For, by myself, I know
We cannot till life's evening keep
The flowers that on its dewy steep
    At earliest dawn did blow.

Yet, lingering round this hallow'd spot,
I call them, though they answer not,
    For some have gone their way,
To sleep that sleep which none may break,
Until the resurrection wake
    The prisoners from their clay.

But thou, most fair and fitful stream,
First prompter of my musing dream,
    Still lovingly dost smile,
And, heedless of the conflict hoarse
With the rude rocks that bar thy course,
    My lonely walk beguile.

Still thou art changed, my favourite scene!
For man hath stolen thy cliffs between,
And torn thy grassy sod;
And bade the intrusive mill-wheel dash,
And many a ponderous engine crash,
Where Nature dream'd of God.

Yet to the spot where first we drew
Our breath, we turn unchanged and true,
As to a nurse's breast;
And count it, e'en till hoary age,
The Mecca of our pilgrimage,
Of all the earth most blest.

And so, thou cataract, strangely wild,
My own loved Yantic's wayward child,
That still dost foam and start;
Though slight thou art, I love thee well,
And, pleased, the lay thy praise doth tell,
Which gushes from the heart.

STRATFORD UPON AVON.

WHAT nurtured Shakspeare mid these village-shades,
Making a poor deer-stalking lad a king
In the broad realm of mind?
                                        I question'd much
Whatever met my view,—the holly-hedge,
The cottage-rose, the roof where he was born,
And the pleach'd avenue of limes that led
To the old church. And, pausing there, I mark'd
The mossy efflorescence on the stones,
Which, kindling in the sunbeam, taught me how
Its little seeds were fed by mouldering life,
And how another race of tiny roots,
The fathers of the future, should compel
From hardest-hearted rocks a nutriment,
Until the fern-plant and the ivy sere
Made ancient buttress and grim battlement
Their nursing-mothers.
                                        But again I ask'd,
"What nurtured Shakspeare?" The rejoicing birds

Wove a wild song, whose burden seem'd to be,
He was their pupil when he chose, and knew
Their secret maze of melody to wind,
Snatching its sweetness for his winged strain
With careless hand.
                    The timid flowerets said,
"He came among us like a sleepless bee,
And all those pure and rarest essences,
Concocted by our union with the skies,
Which in our cups or zones we fain would hide,
He rifled for himself and bore away."

—The winds careering in their might replied,
"Upon our wings he rode, and visited
The utmost stars. We could not shake him off.
E'en on the fleecy clouds he laid his hand,
As on a courser's mane, and made them work
With all their countless hues his wondrous will."

And then meek Avon raised a murmuring voice,
What time the Sabbath chimes came pealing sweet
Through the umbrageous trees, and told how oft
Along those banks he wander'd, pacing slow,
As if to read the depths.
                    Ere I had closed
My questioning, the ready rain came down,

And every pearl-drop as it kiss'd the turf
Said, "We have been his teachers. When we fell
Pattering among the vine leaves, he would list
Our lessons as a student, nor despise
Our simplest lore."
And then the bow burst forth,
That strong love-token of the Deity
Unto a drowning world. Each prismed ray
Had held bright dalliance with the bard, and help'd
To tint the robe in which his thought was wrapp'd
For its first cradle-sleep.
Then twilight came
In her gray robe, and told a tender tale
Of his low musings, while she noiseless drew
Her quiet curtain. And the queenly moon,
Riding in state upon her silver car,
Confess'd she saw him oft, through checkering shades,
Hour after hour, with Fancy by his side,
Linking their young imaginings, like chains
Of pearl and diamond.
Last, the lowly grave—
Shakspeare's own grave—sent forth a hollow tone,
"The heart within my casket *read itself*,
And from that inward wisdom learn'd to scan
The hearts of other men. It ponder'd long
Amid those hermit cells where thought is born,

Explored the roots of passion, and the founts
Of sympathy, and at each seal'd recess
Knock'd, until mystery fled. Hence her loved bard
Nature doth crown with flowers of every hue
And every season; and the human soul,
Owning his power, shall at his magic touch
Shudder, or thrill, while age on age expires."

MIDNIGHT THOUGHTS AT SEA.

BORNE upon the ocean's foam,
Far from native land and home,
Midnight's curtain, dense with wrath,
Brooding o'er our venturous path,
While the mountain wave is rolling,
And the ship's bell faintly tolling:
Saviour! on the boisterous sea,
Bid us rest secure in Thee.

Blast and surge, conflicting hoarse,
Sweep us on with headlong force;
And the bark, which tempests urge,
Moans and trembles at their scourge:
Yet, should wildest tempests swell,
Be thou near, and all is well.
Saviour! on the stormy sea,
Let us find repose in Thee.

Hearts there are with love that burn
When to us afar they turn;
Eyes that show the rushing tear
If our utter'd names they hear:
Saviour! o'er the faithless main,
Bring us to those homes again,
As the trembler, touch'd by Thee,
Safely trod the treacherous sea.

Wrecks are darkly spread below,
Where with lonely keel we go;
Gentle brows and bosoms brave
Those abysses richly pave:
If beneath the briny deep
We, with them, should coldly sleep,
Saviour! o'er the whelming sea,
Take our ransom'd souls to Thee.

THE TRIAL OF THE DEAD.

The solemn mockery of the trial of the dead, which was first permitted in Scotland about the fourteenth century, was exhibited in the case of George Gordon, Earl of Huntley, in the year 1664. After this judicial process, the body was removed from Holyrood, and interred at Elgin Cathedral, the burial-place of his family.

THE spears at Corrichie were bright,
Where, with a stern command,
The Earl of Huntley ranged his host
Upon their native strand.

From many a Highland strath and glen
They at his summons came,
A stalwart band of fearless men,
Who counted war a game.

Then, from Edina's royal court
Fierce Murray northward sped,
And rush'd his envied foe to meet
In battle sharp and dread.

They met, they closed, they struggled sore,
  Like waves when tempests blow,
The slogan-music high in air,
  The sound of groans below.

They broke, they wheel'd, they charged again,
  Till on the ensanguined ground
The noble Gordon lifeless lay,
  Transpierced with many a wound.

Long from her tower his Lady look'd:
  "I see a dusky cloud,
And there, behold! comes floating high
  Earl Huntley's banner proud."

Then, deep she sigh'd, for rising mist
  Involved her aching sight;
'Twas but an autumn-bough that mock'd
  Her chieftain's pennon bright.

His mother by the ingle sate,
  Her head upon her knee,
And murmur'd low in hollow tone,
  "He'll ne'er come back to thee."

"Hist, Lady, mother! hear I not
Steed-tramp and pibroch-roar?
As when the victor-surf doth tread
Upon a rocky shore?"

Not toward the loop-hole raised her head
That woman wise and hoar,
But whisper'd in her troubled soul,
"Thy Lord returns no more!"

"A funeral march is in my ear,
A scatter'd host I see,"
And, straining wild, her sunken eye
Gazed out on vacancy.

Back to their homes, the Gordon clan
Stole with despairing tread,
While to the vaults of Holyrood
Was borne their chieftain dead.

Exulting foemen bore him there,
While lawless vassals jeer'd,
Nor spared to mock the haughty brow
Whose living frown they fear'd.

No earth upon his corse they strew'd,
At no rich shrine inurn'd,
But heavenward, as the warrior fell,
His noble forehead turn'd.

Months fled; and while, from castled height
To cot in lowly dell,
O'er Corrichie's disastrous day
The tears of Scotland fell,

Behold, a high and solemn court
With feudal pomp was graced,
And at the bar, in princely robes,
A muffled chieftain placed.

No glance his veiled face might scan,
Though throngs beside him prest;
The Gordon plume his brow adorn'd,
Its tartan wrapp'd his breast.

"Lord George of Gordon, Huntley's earl!
High-treason taints thy name;
For God, and for thy country's cause,
Defend thine ancient fame;

"Make oath upon thine honour's seal,
  Heaven's truth unblenching tell!"
No lip he moved, no hand he raised,
  And dire that silence fell.

No word he spake, though thrice adjured;
  Then came the sentence drear:
"Foul traitor to thy queen and realm,
  Our laws denounce thee here."

They stripp'd him of his cloak of state,
  They bared his helmed head,
Though the pale judges inly quaked
  Before the ghastly dead.

Light thing to him, that earthly doom
  Or man's avenging rod,
Who, in the land of souls, doth bide
  The audit of his God.

Before his face the crowd drew back,
  As from sepulchral gloom,
And sternest veterans shrank to breathe
  The vapour of the tomb.

And now, this mockery of the dead
  With hateful pageant o'er,
They yield him to his waiting friends
  Who throng the palace door.

And on their sad procession press'd,
  Unresting day and night,
To where mid Elgin's towers they mark
  The fair cathedral's height.

And there, by kindred tears bedew'd,
  Beneath its hallow'd shade,
With midnight torch and chanted dirge,
  Their fallen chief they laid,

Fast by king Duncan's mouldering dust,
  Whose locks of silver hue
Were stain'd, as Avon's swan hath sung,
  With murder's bloody dew.

So, rest thou here, thou Scottish earl
  Of ancient fame and power,
No more a valiant host to guide
  In battle's stormy hour.

Yea, rest thee here, thou Scottish earl,
  Until that day of dread,
Which to eternity consigns
  The trial of the dead.

THE EMIGRANT MOTHER.

FROM my own native clime, I took my way
Across the foaming deep. My husband slept
In his new grave, and poverty had stripp'd
Our lonely cottage. Letters o'er the wave,
From brother and from sister, bade me come
To this New World, where there is bread for all.
So, with my heavy, widow'd heart I went,
My only babe and I.
                                        Coarse, curious eyes
Look'd searchingly upon me, as I sat
In the throng'd steerage, with my sick, sick soul.
But at each jeering word, I bow'd my head
Down o'er my helpless child, and was content,
For he was all my world.
                                        Storms rock'd the bark,
And haggard fear sprang up, with oaths and cries.
Yet wondrous courage nerved me. For to die
With that fair, loving creature in my arms,
Seem'd more than life without him. If a shade

Of weariness or trouble mark'd my brow,
He look'd upon me with his father's eyes,
And I was comforted.
But sickness came,
Close air, and scanty food. Darkly they press'd
On feeble infancy, and oft I heard,
As mournful twilight settled o'er the sea,
The frequent plunge, and the wild mother's shriek,
When her lost darling to the depths went down.
Then came the terror. To my heaving breast
I closer clasp'd the child, and all my strength
Went forth in one continued sigh to God.
Scarcely I slept, lest the dire pestilence
Should smite him unawares. E'en when he lay
In peaceful dreams, the smile upon his cheek,
I trembled, lest the dark-wing'd angel breathed
Insidious whispers, luring him away.

It came at last. That dreadful sickness came,
The fever—short and mortal. Midnight's pall
Spread o'er the waters, when his last faint breath
Moisten'd my cheek. Deep in my breaking heart
I shut the mother's cry.
One mighty fear
Absorb'd me, lest his cherish'd form should feed
The dire sea-monsters, nor beneath the sods

Of the green, quiet, blessed earth, await
The resurrection.
So, I shuddering press'd
The body closer, though its deadly cold
Froze through my soul.
To those around, I said,
"Disturb him not—he sleepeth." Then I sang
And rock'd him tenderly, as though he woke
In fretfulness, or felt the sting of pain.
My poor, dead baby! Terrible to me
Such falsehood seem'd. But yet the appalling dread
Lest the fierce, scaly monsters of the sea
Should wind around him with their gorging jaws,
O'ermaster'd me.
Nights fled, and mornings dawn'd,
And still my chill arms clasp'd immovably
The shrivelling form. They told me he was dead,
And bade me give my beautiful to them,
For burial in the deep. With outstretch'd hands
They stood demanding him, until the light
Fled from my swimming eyes.
But when I woke
From the long trance, that icy burden lay
No longer on my bosom. Pitying words
The captain spake—"Look at yon little boat
Lash'd to our stern. There, in his coffin, rests

The body of thy son. If in three days
We reach the land, he shall be buried there
As thou desirest."

There, from breaking morn,
My eyes were fix'd; and when the darkness came
By the red binnacle's uncertain light
I watch'd that floating speck amid the waves,
And pray'd for land.

As thus I kept my watch,
Like desolate Rizpah, mournful visions came
Of my forsaken cottage; while the spring
Of gushing crystal, where 'neath bowering trees
We drew our water, gurgled in my ear
To mock me with its memories of joy.
My throat was dry with anguish, and when voice
Fail'd me to pray for land, I lifted up
That silent, naked thought, which finds the Throne
Sooner than pomp of words.

With fiery face
And eager foot, the third dread morning rose
Out of the misty deep, and coldly rang
The death-knell of my hope.

As o'er the stern
I gazed with dim eye on the flashing brine,
Methought its depths were open'd, and I saw
Creatures most vile, that o'er the bottom crept,

Lizards and slimy serpents, hideous forms
And shapes, for which man's language hath no name;
While to the surface rose the monster shark,
Intent to seize his prey.
                                        Convulsive shrieks,
Long pent within my bleeding heart, burst forth.
But from the watcher at the mast there came
A shout of "*Land!*" and on the horizon's edge
Gleam'd a faint streak, like the white seraph's wing.
Oh! blessed land! We near'd it, and my breath
Was one continued gasp—*Oh! blessed land!*

A boat was launch'd. With flashing oar it reach'd
A lonely isle. Bent o'er the vessel's side,
I saw them dig a narrow grave, and lay
In the cool bosom of the quiet earth
The little body that was mine no more.
Nor wept I: for an angel said to me,
"God's will! God's will! and thy requited prayer
Remember!"
                                To my hand a scroll they brought,
Bearing the name of that deserted strand,
And record of the day in which they laid
My treasure there. They might have spared that toil:
A mother's unforgetful love needs not
Record or date.

The ship held on her course
To greener shores. There came an exile's pain,
Beneath a foreign sky.
Yet 'twere a sin
To mourn with bitterness the boy whose smile
Cheers me no more, since the sea had him not,
Nor the sea-monsters.
Endless praise to Him,
Who did not scorn the poor, weak woman's sigh
Of desolate wo.
No monument is thine,
Oh babe! that 'neath yon sterile sands dost sleep,
Save the strong sculpture in a mother's heart;
And by those traces will she know thee well
When the graves open, and before God's throne
Both small and great are gather'd.

HEALING AT SUNSET.

"At even, when the sun did set, they brought unto him all that were diseased."
MARK i. 32.

JUDEA'S summer-day went down,
And lo! from vale and plain,
Around the heavenly Healer throng'd
A sick and sorrowing train.

The pallid brow, the hectic cheek,
The cripple bent with care,
And he whose soul dark demons lash'd
To foaming rage, were there.

He raised his hand, the lame man leap'd,
The blind forgot his wo,
And with a startling rapture gazed
On Nature's glorious show.

Up from his bed of misery rose
The paralytic pale,
While the loathed leper dared once more
His fellow-man to hail.

The lunatic's illumined brow,
  With smiles of love o'erspread,
Assured the kindred hearts that long
  Had trembled at his tread.

The mother to her idiot-boy
  The name of Jesus taught,
Who thus with sudden touch had fired
  The chaos of his thought.

Yes, all that sad, imploring train
  He heal'd ere evening fell,
And speechless joy was born that night
  In many a lonely cell.

Ere evening fell! Oh ye, who find
  The chills of age descend,
And with the lustre of your locks
  The almond-blossom blend;

Haste, ere the darkening shades of night
  Have every hope bereaved,
Nor leave the safety of the soul
  Unstudied, unachieved.

FILIAL PIETY OF DAVID.

ADULLAM'S sheltering cavern bent
O'er many an exile's head,
Who from the tyrant sway of Saul
In discontent had fled;
And he, the leader of that band,
Came forth in sadden'd thought,
And to a foreign monarch's court
His suit a suppliant brought:

"Oh, King of Moab!" bowing down
With trembling lip he said
Who oft to victory's crimson field
Had Israel's thousands led,
"I pray thee, let mine aged sire,
And she beside whose knee
My earliest, lisping prayer was learn'd,
In safety dwell with thee.

"Lest, while the adverse torrent's force
With struggling breast I stem,
My hands grow weak, my spirits faint,
In anxious care for them;
For with an outlaw's ceaseless pain,
I wander to and fro,
And wait Jehovah's righteous will
More perfectly to know."

Then forth to Moab's pitying prince
His aged sire he led,
The cavern dampness on the locks
That silver'd o'er his head;
And, leaning on his vigorous arm,
A wrinkled woman came,
The mother of the many sons
Who honour'd Jesse's name.

The youngest and the dearest one
Now woke her parting tear,
And sorrow shook his manly breast
That ne'er had quail'd with fear;
While, drawing near the monarch's side,
In low and earnest tone
He press'd upon his soften'd heart
The treasures of his own.

Low kneeling at his parent's side,
  That blessing he besought,
Which ever in his childish years
  Had calm'd each troubled thought;
While they with fond and feeble hand
  His clustering curls among,
Jehovah's majesty and might
  Invoked with faltering tongue.

With tearful thanks to Moab's king,
  The exile left the place,
For filial duty well discharged
  Shed sunshine o'er his face;
And sweet as when on Bethlehem's vales
  He fed his fleecy flock,
The dew of holy song distill'd
  Like honey from the rock.

"God is my light! Why should I fear,
  Though earth be dark with shade?
God is the portion of my soul,
  Why should I be afraid?
Unless his arm had been my stay
  When snares were round me spread,
My strength had fainted and gone down
  To silence and the dead.

"Father and mother, dear and true
  The homeless one forsake,
While like the hunted deer, my course
  From cliff to cliff I take.
Though kings against my life conspire,
  And hosts in hate array'd,
God is the portion of my soul;
  Why should I be afraid?"

THE IVY.

Beautiful plant, clasping the ruin'd tower
That Time hath wreck'd, and venturing fearless up
Into the frosty sky! hast thou a heart
For constant friendship, that thou thus dost dare
Peril, and storm, and winter's tyranny,
With changeless brow?

The lonely shaft that falls
From its high place, thou in thy helpful arms
Dost wind embracing, its disjointed stones
Knitting with thy strong root-work, like a mesh
Of living nerves.

The brown and gnarled trunk,
Whose heart the worm hath eaten, thou dost deck
As for its bridal, hiding every seam
And wrinkle with thy broider'd drapery.
The broken column mid the desert sands,
Where dim antiquity hath dozed so long
That slow oblivion stole the date away
Which history seeks in vain, thou still dost gird

And cherish as a tender wife, who loves
Best when all else forsake.
'Twas sweet to sit
Beneath thy shade, and mark thee closely wrap
The castellated domes of the old world;
For though within no habitants were found,
Save noisome bats, or the gray, boding owl,
Uttering her nightly shriek, yet thou untired
Didst do thy pleasant work of charity,
Feeding the glad birds with thy berries sere,
That thickly nested mid thy niches green.
Art thou a Christian, Ivy,—thus to clothe
The naked, and the broken heart to bind,
And bless the old, and cheer the desolate?
A teacher sure thou art, and shouldst be rank'd
Among the few who by example teach,
Making a text-book of their own strong heart
And blameless life.
And should we linger here,
Till our props fall around us, and each rose
Fades in our grasp, oh! might one friend remain,
Fond and unchanged like thee; we scarce should heed
The touch of wasting time.
Yea, should some stone
Or funeral column chronicle our name,
Stretch out thine arms, and wreathe it, reaching forth

Thy freshly lustrous leaf, and showing all
The young who wander there, how to be true
In love, and pitiful to wo, and kind
To hoary age, and with unswerving heart
Do good to those who render naught again.

THE RAINBOW.

Mountain! that first received the foot of man,
Giving him shelter when the shoreless flood
That whelm'd a buried world went surging by,
I see thee in thy lonely grandeur rise;
I see the white-hair'd Patriarch, as he knelt
Beside his earthen altar mid his sons,
While beat in praise the only pulse of life
Upon this buried planet.—O'er the gorged
And furrow'd soil swept forth a numerous train,
Horned, or cloven-footed, fierce or tame,
While, mix'd with song, the sound of countless wings,
His rescued prisoners, fann'd the ambient air.

The sun drew near his setting, clothed in gold,
But on the Patriarch, ere from prayer he rose,
A darkly-cinctured cloud chill tears had wept,
And rain-drops lay upon his silver hairs.
Then burst an arch of wondrous radiance forth,
Spanning the vaulted skies. Its mystic scroll

Proclaim'd the amnesty that pitying heaven
Granted to earth, all desolate and void.

Oh signet-ring! with which the Almighty seal'd
His treaty with the remnant of the clay
That shrank before him, to remotest time
Stamp wisdom on the souls that turn to thee.
Sublime Instructor! who four thousand years
Hast ne'er withheld thy lesson, but unfurl'd,
As shower and sunbeam bade, thy glorious scroll,
Oft, mid the summer's day, I musing sit
At my lone casement, to be taught of thee.
Born of the tear-drop and the smile, methinks,
Thou hast affinity with man, for such
His elements and pilgrimage below.
Our span of strength and beauty fades like thine,
Yet stays its fabric on eternal truth
And boundless mercy.
The wild floods may come,
The everlasting fountains burst their bounds,
The exploring dove without a leaf return,
Yea, the fires glow that melt the solid rock,
And earth be wreck'd: *What then?* Be still, my soul;
Enter thine ark; God's promise cannot fail;
For surely as yon rainbow tints the cloud,
His truth, thine Ararat, will shelter thee.

THE THRIVING FAMILY.

A SONG.

OUR father lives in Washington,
  And has a world of cares,
But gives his children each a farm,
  Enough for them and theirs.
Full thirty well grown sons has he,
  A numerous race indeed,
Married and settled all, d'ye see,
  With boys and girls to feed.
So if we wisely till our lands,
  We're sure to earn a living,
And have a penny, too, to spare
  For spending or for giving.
A thriving family are we,
  No lordling need deride us,
For we know how to use our hands,
  And in our wits we pride us.
    Hail, brothers, hail,
  Let nought on earth divide us.

Some of us dare the sharp north-east;
  Some, clover fields are mowing;
And others tend the cotton plants
  That keep the looms a-going;
Some build and steer the white-wing'd ships,
  And few in speed can mate them,
While others rear the corn and wheat,
  Or grind the corn to freight them.
And if our neighbours o'er the sea
  Have e'er an empty larder,
To send a loaf their babes to cheer
  We'll work a little harder.
No old nobility have we,
  No tyrant king to ride us;
Our sages in the Capitol
  Enact the laws that guide us.
    Hail, brothers, hail,
  Let nought on earth divide us.

Some faults we have, we can't deny,
  A foible here and there;
But other households have the same,
  And so we won't despair.
'Twill do no good to fume and frown,
  And call hard names, you see,

And what a shame 'twould be to part
So fine a family!
'Tis but a waste of time to fret,
Since Nature made us one,
For every quarrel cuts a thread
That healthful Love has spun.
Then draw the cords of union fast,
Whatever may betide us,
And closer cling through every blast,
For many a storm has tried us.
Hail, brothers, hail,
Let nought on earth divide us.

THE VICTIM OF THE DEEP.

Unfathom'd main! who to thy dark embrace
Hast taken the born of earth, the varied haunts
Of his young boyhood's sport, the corn-clad fields
Where erst he held the plough, remember him.
Home and its many voices, wild with grief,
Reproach thee for his absence, and demand
Why he returns not.

For with vigorous step
He left his cottage-door. Through his young veins
The health-tide coursed, and in each compact limb
Strength revell'd. And with such confiding joy
He turn'd to thee, that scarce a mother's wo
Woke one brief tear.

Who whispereth he is dead?
Dead! And how died he?

Answer us, thou Sea!
No doubt, thou fain wouldst hide the fearful tale,
The plunge, the gasp, the agonizing pang
With which thy treacherous policy was seal'd.

What right hadst thou, without one sound of knell,
Or hallow'd prayer, or step of funeral train,
In thy cold-hearted heathenism to take
Him on whose brow the pure baptismal dew
Was shed, which mark'd him of the fold of Christ?
E'en now thou roll'st above him, with the play
Of all thy crested waves, mocking the trust
Which, from the footing of the firm, green earth,
He drew to place on thee.

His boyish eye
Thou lur'dst with pictures of the snowy sail
Swelling in beauty, of the foreign port
Replete with wealth, and of the glowing scene
Of glad return. How hast thou kept thy pledge,
Devouring main?

Oh! break thy sullen pause,
And tell us how he died.

The storm was high,
And, wrapp'd in midnight, mid the slippery shroud
He miss'd his footing. Loose he swang and wide
Over the boiling surge, a single rope
Grasping convulsively, and on the blast
Pouring wild cries for help.

The strain'd ship lurch'd,
And from the billows rose a voice of prayer
Unto redeeming love. A rope was cast,

Yet he beheld it not; a life-boat lower'd,
But the shrill echo of his comrades' shout
Sank 'neath the tumult of the thunder-blast,
And cold death-silence settled where he strove
Briefly, with panting breast.
Relentless Sea!
Doth it not grieve thee, that a broken heart
Sinks heavy in a mother's breast for this?
Or that a pale-brow'd maiden counts the hours,
By sound of dropping tears?
But there shall come
A blast of trumpet, and thy startled depths
All the reft spoil of earth shall render back,
Atom by atom.
Then mayst thou arise
In glorious beauty, Sailor-Boy! and meet
That Saviour's smile, whose name was on thy lip
When broke the last wave o'er thee.
Mayst thou hear
His blessed welcome to a peaceful home
Where there is no more sea.

HAROLD AND TOSTI.

Tosti, a son of Earl Godwin, joined Hardrada, king of Norway, in an invasion of England, his native land, and fought against his brother Harold, the last of the Saxon monarchs, at the battle of Stamford-Bridge, September 25th, 1066.

On England's shore, the pirate king
Of Norway's frigid clime,
From thrice a hundred beaked ships,
Debark'd his men of crime;
While at his side the outlaw son
Of proud Earl Godwin came,
And many a child in terror shrank
At dreaded Tosti's name.

King Harold led a dauntless host,
For every loyal thane,
Arousing at his country's call,
Convoked a vassal-train;
And while green Autumn robed the vales,
And corn was waving high,
Those vengeful armies frowning met,
Where Derwent murmur'd by.

But England's power, in mass compact,
  Was ranged o'er hill and dale,
Solemn, and motionless, and dark,
  A mountain clothed in mail.
Then Harold paused a moment's space,
  Ere shafts in blood were dyed,
And of Earl Edwin ask'd, who rode
  In armour by his side,—

"Who wears yon scarf of azure dye,
  And helm of burnish'd gold?"
"Hardrada, prince of Norway's realm,
  A warrior fierce and bold."
"And who is he, with towering head,
  Majestic, firm, and cool,
Who casts around such eagle-glance,
  As he the world would rule?"

"The rebel of Earl Godwin's line;"
  Yet spared the words to speak,
Thy brother, for he saw the blood
  Forsake his sovereign's cheek;
And though he rein'd his prancing steed,
  His brow was pale as clay,
That brow which ne'er had blanch'd before
  In battle's deadliest fray.

Fraternal memories o'er his heart
  Like softening waters flow'd,—
The mother's kiss, the mother's prayer,
  Alike on both bestow'd.
Then parted from his armed ranks
  A knight of noble mien,
And waved a snowy flag of truce
  Those frowning hosts between.

"To Tosti, great Earl Godwin's son,
  King Harold bids me say,
Why standst thou on thy native soil
  Amid its foes this day?
I yield thee all Northumbria's realm,
  The choicest of my land;
Lay down thine arms, disperse thy host,
  And clasp a brother's hand."

But Tosti turned to Norway's king:
  "Behold my friend," said he;
"What is thy monarch's boon for him
  If such his gifts to me?"
"Thus Harold answereth Norway's lord,
  Troubler of earth and wave;
Just seven good feet of English soil
  I yield thee for a grave."

Then Tosti shouted, loud and wild,
He smote his buckler proud,
And spears and lances flash'd amain,
Like lightning from the cloud;
And England's mail-clad cavalry
Rush'd on, with direst shock,
As strikes old Ocean's stormy surge
Against the fissured rock.

Then calmly from the English lines
Rode forth a mitred thane,
Wulstan,* the bishop, wise and old,
Of Worcester's sacred fane;
Though scarce the impetuous tide of war
Held back its panting wave,
While thus that white-hair'd man of peace
His sovereign's message gave:

"Oh, Tosti! by the memory dear
Of boyhood's early trace,
When thou wert victor at the ring,
And foremost in the chase,

---

* Wulstan, the venerable Bishop of Worcester, had previously accompanied King Harold into Northumberland, where a violent insurrection was quelled, without an appeal to the sword, by the influence of his eloquence and piety. He was one of the most revered of the prelates, whom the early Saxon chroniclers were accustomed to designate as *mass-thanes*, to distinguish them from the barons, or *world-thanes*.

And by our parent's blessed love,
  That still its vigil kept,
When, cheek to cheek, and heart to heart,
  On the same couch we slept;

"E'en by the mercies of our Lord,
  Who for our sins did die,
Spare the dire waste of blood, and take
  A brother's clemency."
"Speed back, speed back, thou Saxon kern!
  And, if thy steed be slow,
The swift-wing'd darts of glorious strife
  May chance to lay thee low."

And with the rebel's echoed ire,
  A tide of crimson rolls,
With clang of shield and cloven helm,
  And cry of parting souls.
Nor stay'd that deadly passion-strife,
  Till o'er the ensanguined plain
The flying Northmen wail'd their kind,
  With haughty Tosti slain.

Yet Harold, mid that triumph hour,
  His tent in sadness sought,

And deem'd the victory all too dear
  A brother's blood had bought:
While, on that field, the bleaching bones
  For many a year did tell,
Where Peace the angel strove in vain
  The demon War to quell.

THE CLOCK AT VERSAILLES.

In the palace of Versailles, a clock, during the whole life of the reigning monarch, pointed with its motionless hands to the hour when his predecessor died, and was only to be again moved at the moment of his own death.

WHERE the halls with splendour glow,
Where the gorgeous fountains throw
        Fullest flood,
There a chrônicler of time,
Wrapp'd in mystery sublime,
        Mutely stood.

Like the finger on the wall
That Belshazzar's festival
        Dash'd with dread,
Stern it bore the doom of fate,
While the crowd with joy elate
        Check'd their tread.

Fix'd as adamantine chain,
Wilt thou never move again?

Then methought an inward strain
Murmur'd low,
"Blind with pomp or folly's chase
Call the king! He can trace
The true answer in my face,
He doth know.

"When he struggleth long and sore,
When he links to earth no more
Hate or love,
When his eye hath lost its light,
When his hands grow stiff and white,
Mine shall move.

"When his crown availeth not,
And the death-hues blear and blot
Brow and cheek,
When his tongue no more can frame
Vaunt of power or moan of shame,
Mine shall speak.

"I shall speak—I shall move,
While his fickle courtiers rove
Far away;
With my doom of fate and fear

For the new-made monarch's ear
I shall stay."

Slow the murmur in the breast
Died away, and there at rest,
Still and stern,
Stood that monitor sublime,
Teaching truths that power and prime
Shrink to learn.

THE PRINCE OF EDOM.

1 Kings xi. 21.

THE warriors of David came down in their ire,
And Edom was scathed with their deluge of fire;
O'er the wrecks of its throne roll'd oblivion's dark flood,
And the thirst of its valleys was satiate with blood.

Its prince, a lone outcast, an orphan distrest,
In the palace of Egypt found refuge and rest,
And the queen's gentle sister, with eye like the dove,
Became in her beauty the bride of his love.

Yet still, a dark shade o'er his features would stray,
Though the lute-strings thrill'd soft and the banquet was gay;
For the land of his fathers in secret he pined,
And murmur'd his grief to the waves and the wind.

"The voice of my country! it haunteth my dreams,
I start from my sleep at the rush of its streams;
Oh, monarch of Egypt! sole friend in my wo,
I would see it once more. Let me go! let me go!"

"Wouldst thou hie to the desert, and couch with the bear?
Or the lion disturb in his desolate lair?
Wouldst thou camp on the ruins with brambles o'ergrown
While the blasts in their mockery respond to thy moan?

"Know'st thou not that the sword of stern Joab was red
Till the dukes of Idumea were slaughter'd and dead?
Know'st thou not that his vengeance relax'd not, nor stay'd
Till six moons wax'd and waned o'er the carnage he made?"

"I know that our roof-trees in ashes were laid,
And the vine and the olive hew'd down from each glade;
Yet still some pale sprouts from their roots may be seen,
And the clefts of the rock with their foliage be green.

"I know that our virgins, so stately and fair,
Who wreathed with the pearl and the topaz their hair,
That our merchants, whose wealth with a monarch's has vied
In Phœnicia and Zidon in bondage abide.

"But roused by my trumpet, the captives shall haste
From the far, foreign realms, where their life-blood they waste;
From the walls of Azotus with speed they shall fly,
And nest, like the bird, 'neath their own native sky."

"O prince of red Edom, content thee, be still;
Of the treasures of Egypt partake at thy will;
See, thy wife lights thy bower with the wealth of her charms,
And thy babe, as she names thee, leaps high in her arms.

"Thou know'st from thy realm all the people have fled,
That the friends of thy childhood are cold with the dead;
Every drop of thy blood from that region is reft,
No voice of thy kindred to welcome thee left."

"Let me go, king of Egypt, to visit my slain,
To weep o'er their dust, who revive not again;
Though nought in their courts save the lizard should glide,
And the bat flap his wing in their chambers of pride,

"Yet still shall Mount Seir in his grandeur remain,
Still the rivers roll on to the fathomless main,
If no tone of the living should solace my wo,
To the land of my birth, let me go, let me go."

THE WISH OF THE WEARY WOMAN.

A FORM there was, still spared by time
Till the slow century fill'd its prime;
Stretch'd on its bed, with half-closed eye
It mark'd uncertain shades flit by;
Nor scarce the varied world of sound
To the seal'd ear admittance found;
While the worn brow, in wrinkles dark,
Seem'd like the gnarl'd oak's roughen'd bark.

Oh! e'er did youthful beauty deck
Those wither'd limbs, yon living wreck?
Did blushes o'er that leathern cheek
The warmth of wild emotion speak?
Did rosy health that lip bedew,
And kneeling love for favour sue?
Alas! alas! for him who bears
A hundred years earth's load of cares.

'Twere vain to ask, what legends old
That brain might in its chambers hold;
What pictures in its gallery fade,
By Fancy touch'd or Hope portray'd;
For Memory locks the cloister'd cell,
And Silence guards the citadel;
But still that weary woman's eye
Doth gaze and fix on vacancy.

Yet the faint lungs spontaneous play,
The heart's pulsations hold their way,
And helpless to the garden borne,
Or laid beside the blossom'd thorn,
What time the vernal noontide hour
Gave deeper life to shrub and flower,
Methought a quickening influence stole
O'er stagnant veins, and frigid soul.

A knell burst forth! From turret high
Its mournful cadence floated by;
E'en on that rigid ear it broke,
And, strange to say, the tear awoke.
Then lo! a hoarse, sepulchral tone,
As when imprison'd waters moan,
Moved the parch'd lips to utterance free,
"Ah! when will that bell toll for me?

"All, all are gone! the husband dear,
The loving child, the friend sincere.
Once toward their graves with grief I prest,
But now I bless their dreamless rest;
For lone, amid a stranger-band,
Sad relic of the past I stand;
Dead at the root, a blasted tree;
Ah! when will that bell toll for me?

"Hath Death forgotten? To his halls
Childhood and youthful prime he calls;
In bowers of love, or domes of pride,
He finds them, wheresoe'er they hide:
Fain would they 'scape, but to his sight
I hasten, and his shaft invite.
Hath God forgot? I bend the knee,
Oh, let that knell be toll'd for me!"

THE FIRST MISSIONARY.

KNOW'ST thou the Leader of that band who toil
The everlasting gospel's light to shed
On earth's benighted climes?

Canst tell the name
Of the first Teacher in whose steps went forth,
O'er sultry India, and the sea-green isles,
And to the forest children of the West,
A self-denying band, who counted not
Life dear unto them, so they might fulfil
Their ministry, and save the heathen soul?

Judea's mountains from their breezy heights
Reply, "We heard him when he lifted up
His voice, and taught the people patiently
Line upon line, for they were slow of heart."
From its dark depths the Galilean lake
Told hoarsely to the storm-cloud, how he dealt
Bread to the famish'd throng with tender care,
Forgetting not the body, while he fed

The immortal spirit; how he stood and heal'd
Day after day, till evening shadows fell
Around the pale and paralytic train,
Lame, halt, and blind, and lunatic, who sought
His pitying touch.

Mount Olivet in sighs
Spake mournfully, "His midnight prayer was mine;
I heard it, I alone, as all night long
Upward it rose, with tears for those who paid
His love with hatred."

Kedron's slender rill
That bathed his feet, as to his lowly work
Of mercy he went forth, still kept his name
Securely hoarded in its secret fount,
A precious pearl-drop!

Sad Gethsemane
Had memories that it falter'd to repeat,
Such as the strengthening angel mark'd appall'd,
Finding no dialect in which to bear
Their wo to heaven.

E'en Calvary, who best
Might, if it would, our earnest question solve,
Press'd close its flinty lip, and shuddering bow'd
In silent dread, remembering how the sun
Grew dark at noonday, and the sheeted dead

Came from their mouldering sepulchres, to walk
Among the living.
                                        But the bold bad host,
Spirits of evil, from the lake of pain,
Who held brief triumph round the mystic cross,
Bare truthful witness, as they shrieking fled,
"We know thee who thou art, the Christ of God:"
While heaven, uplifting its eternal gates,
With chant of cherubim and seraphim,
Welcomed the Lord of glory entering in,
His mission done.

"SORROW AS ON THE SEA."

Jeremiah.

"*Sorrow as on the sea.*"

O man of grief,
Prophet! who in the troublous time of siege
And famine, when the fierce Chaldean bands
Invaded Israel, didst predict her fate
And feel her vengeance, didst thou ever taste
The sorrow of the sea? Strength reft away,
The spirit melted, hope in darkness lost,
And that eternal loathing, day by day,
Born of those cruel tossings that forbid
The tortured nerve upon its rack to rest,—
For these, thy plaintive harp, that sang so well
Of prison woes, must strike another string.

Thunder upon the main!

Ho, mariner,
For whom the landsman in his happy home
Hath little feeling, mount the shrouds, go up

Into the inky blackness, dare the shaft
Of heaven's red lightning on the pointed mast,
Speck as thou art, which neither sea nor sky
Own, or remember, mid their maniac strife.
The good ship breasts the surge, intent to bide
The battle bravely. Yet, like hunted deer,
It croucheth in the hollow of the sea,
Until the full-mouthed billows drive it forth
Reeling and scathed. Anon, the madden'd winds
Pour out fresh forces, and with riven crest
It rusheth desperate o'er the terraced wave,
Vex'd by their dread artillery. O hearts
Of human mould! that, soften'd by the love
Of home and kindred, have endured the scourge
Of Ocean's tempests, or upon the wreck,
Week after week, held with untold despair
Gaunt fellowship, ye might a tale unfold
To daunt the dream, and turn the revel pale.

Sorrow as on the sea!

A woman mourns,
Pale as the little marble form she folds
Close in her arms, resisting all who touch
The darling of her bosom.

"'Twill awake;
It hath but fainted. The wild, rocking sea

Hath made it sick. I tell ye 'twill revive.
Child! baby! look on me! 'Twill smile again."
"Yes, mother, yes! but not below the skies."
Spasm and convulsion seize her at the thought
That the dear idol, whom but yesterday
She cradled from the zephyr's roughen'd breath,
Alone must to the unfathom'd depths go down,
And for its little body find a bed
Amid the scaly monsters of the deep.
Yet so it is. And she must wend her way
O'er the stern waves that made her desolate,
To her far home again, having let fall
Her soul's chief jewel in the trackless deep.

Sorrow as on the sea!
Ye know it not
Who feel a firm foundation 'neath your feet,
And sleep, unvex'd by waves. Death comes indeed,
But smites you in the sacred place of graves,
Where ye may lay your dead with solemn knell
And tender sympathies of funeral train,
And duly visit them, and dress their couch
With blessed flowers, type of their rising day.
Yea, from the gray-hair'd sexton on his spade,
Bespeak your own turf-pillow where to lie,
And rest beside them, when in God's good time

The pale death-angel comes to summon thee.
True, there is grief on earth. But when ye drain
Its cup of bitterness, give thanks to God
If, in your pilgrimage, ye ne'er have known
The sorrow of the sea.

OUR COUNTRY.

Land of broad rivers and of ocean-lakes,
Sky-kissing cliffs and prairies prank'd with flowers,
That, seated on thy mountain-throne, dost hear
The Atlantic and Pacific's mighty surge
Battling against thy coast, and throw to each
Thy snow-white sails, that visit every clime
And kindred under heaven,—fair land! free land!
How glorious art thou.

Mid thy cultured vales
The sturdy reapers sing, garnering the corn
That feedeth other realms besides their own.
—Toil lifts his brawny arm, and takes the wealth
That makes his children princes; Learning wins
By studious lamp the better gold, that dreads
Nor rust nor robber's wile; Art deftly brings
Tissue and tincture and the fretted stone;
Strange steeds of iron, with their ceaseless freight,
Tramp night and day; while the red lightning bears
Thy slightest whisper on its wondrous wing.

—Proudly thou spread'st thine eagle-pinion o'er
The exiled, and the crush'd from every clime,
Giving them welcome. May no vulture beak
Transpierce thee for thine hospitality,
But sons of strangers build thy walls, and call
Thy gates salvation.

'Neath thy lofty dome
'Tis good to linger, where, in conclave high,
Convene the chosen from thy many States,
Sages, and men of eloquence, who stretch
Their line of travel through an empire's length
To pour their wisdom at thy shrine, and make
Thy union perfect. From the wind-swept hills,
To where the rich magnolia drinks the breath
Of fervid suns—from the great, beating heart
Of the young, giant West, to where the East,
Wrinkled with thought, doth nurse a nation's mind,
They come to do thee honour. There, to list
The grave debate, or catch the kindling thrill
With which impassion'd eloquence maintains
Thine equal laws, inspires the ardent prayer
Of patriot love, that God would hold thee safe,
And firmly knit thy children's hearts, to share
One home, one destiny.

A mighty wind
Doth shake the palaces of ancient time,

And voices mid the despot thrones are heard,
Crying, as in Jerusalem of old,
"Let us depart!" But thou, my blessed land,
Like some fair hearth which hovering angels guard,
Gather thine offspring round thee, and make bright
Their hallow'd chain of love. Warn them to bear
Each other's burdens, seek the common good,
Be pitiful to error, and repress
Each ruder breath that stirs to wrathful deeds.

Oh, beautiful and glorious! thou dost wrap
The robes of Liberty around thy breast,
And as a matron watch thy little ones
Who from their cradle seek the village school,
Bearing the baptism on their infant brow
Of Christian faith and knowledge, like the bud
That, at the bursting of its sheath, doth feel
Pure dews, and heavenward turn.
There is thy strength,
In thy young children, and in those who lead
Their souls to righteousness. The mother's prayer
With her sweet lisper, ere it sinks to rest—
The faithful teacher mid a plastic group—
The classic halls—the hamlet's slender spire
From whence, as from the solemn gothic pile
That crowns the city's pomp, ascendeth sweet

Jehovah's praise—these are thy strength, my land!
These are thy hope.
Oh! lonely ark, that rid'st
A tossing deluge, dark with history's wrecks,
And paved with dead who made not Heaven their help,
God keep thee perfect in thy many parts,
Bound in one living whole.

REMOVAL OF AN ANCIENT MANSION.

WHERE art thou, old friend?
When last
This familiar haunt I past,
Thou didst seem in vigorous cheer,
As like to stand as any here,
With roof-tree firm, and comely face
Well preserved in attic grace,
On columns fair thine arches resting,
Among thy trees the spring-birds nesting;
Hast thou vanished? Can it be
I no more shall gaze on thee?

Casements whence the taper's ray
Glitter'd o'er the crowded way,
Where, embalm'd in fragrant dew,
Peer'd the snowy lilac through;
Chimneys whence the volumed smoke
Of thy warm heart freely spoke;

Fallen and gone! No vestige left,
Stone from stone asunder reft,
While a chasm, with rugged face,
Yawns and darkens in thy place.

Threshold! which I oft have prest,
More a habitant than guest,
For their blessed sakes who shed
Oil of gladness on my head,
Brows with hoary wisdom drest,
Saints who now in glory rest,
Fain had I, though tear-drops fell,
Said to thee one kind farewell;
Fain with tender, grateful sigh,
Thank'd thee for the days gone by.

Hearth-stone! where the ample fire
Quell'd old Winter's fiercest ire,
While its blaze reflected clear
On the friends who gather'd near,
On the pictures quaint and old,
Thou of quiet pleasures told;
Knitting-bag, and storied page,
Precepts grave from lips of age,
Made the lengthen'd evening fleet
Lightly, with improvement sweet.

Fallen dome! beloved so well,
Thou couldst many a legend tell
Of the chiefs, of ancient fame,
Who to share thy shelter came.
Rochambeau and La Fayette
Round thy plenteous board have met,
With Columbia's mightier son,
Great and glorious Washington.
Here with kindred minds they plann'd
Rescue for an infant land,
While the British lion's roar
Echoed round the leaguered shore.

He, who now where cypress weeps,
On Mount Vernon's bosom sleeps,
Once in council grave and high
Shared thy hospitality,
When the sound of treason drear,
Arnold's treason, met his ear.
Heart that ne'er in danger quail'd,
Lips that ne'er had faltered paled,
As the Judas' image stole,
Shuddering, o'er his stainless soul,
And he sped, like tempest's shock,
On to West Point's perill'd rock.

Beauty here, with budding pride,
Blossom'd into youth, and died;
Manhood tower'd with ruling mind,
Age in reverent arms declined,
Bridals bright and burials dread
From thy gates their trains have sped;
But thy lease of time is run,
Closed thy date, thy history done.

All are vanish'd, all have fled,
Save the memories of the dead;
These with added strength adhere
To the hearts that year by year
Feebler beat, and fainter glow,
Till they rest in turf below;
Till their place on earth shall be
Blotted out, old dome, like thee.

Other fanes, 'neath favouring skies,
(Blessings on them!) here may rise;
Other groups, by hope be led,
(Blessings on them!) here to tread;
Yet of thee, their children fair
Nothing wot, and nothing care.
So a form, that soon must be
Number'd with the past like thee,

Rests with pilgrim-staff awhile,
On thy wreck, deserted pile,
And the dust that once was thine
Garners for affection's shrine.

THE LOST LILY.

FAIN would I tell a tale of Wyoming
In days long past. There was a rural home,
Lonely, yet pleasant, near whose door a brook,
Where water-cresses grew, went singing by.
In its small garden, many a cultured bush
Of ripening berries mingled here and there
With spicy herbs, sage and the bee-loved thyme,
While through thick boughs the blushing apple peer'd,
Betokening thrift and comfort.

Once, as closed
The autumn-day, the mother by her side
Held her young children, with her storied lore.
Fast by her chair, a bold and bright-eyed boy
Stood statue-like, while closer, at her feet,
Sate his two gentle sisters. One, a girl
Of some seven summers, youngest, and most loved
For her prolonged and feeble infancy.
She lean'd upon her mother's lap, and look'd
Into her face with an intense regard,

And the quick, intermitting sob that shows
The listening spirit.
Pale she was, and fair,
And so exceeding fragile, that the name
Given by her wilder playmates, at their sports,
Of "Lily of the Vale," seem'd well bestow'd.
The mother told them of her native clime,
Her own, beloved New-England; of the school,
Where many children o'er their lessons bent,
Each mindful of the rules, to read, or spell,
Or ply the needle at the appointed hour;
And how they serious sate, with folded hands,
When the good mistress through her spectacles
Explain'd the Bible.
Of the church she spake,
With snowy spire, by elms o'er-canopied;
And how the sweet bell, on the Sabbath morn,
Summon'd from every home the people forth,
All neatly clad, and with a reverent air,
Children by parents led, to worship God.
Absorb'd in such recital, ever mix'd
By that maternal lip with precepts pure
Of love to God and man, they scarcely mark'd
A darkening shadow o'er the casement steal,
Until the savage footstep and the flash
Of tomahawk appall'd them.

Swift as thought
They fled, through dell and thicket, closely track'd
By grim pursuers. The frail mother, tax'd
With the loved burden of her youngest born,
Moved slowest, and they cleft her fiercely down;
Yet with that impulse which doth sometimes move
The sternest purpose of the red man's breast
To a capricious mercy, spared the child.
Her little struggling limbs, her streaming eyes
Averted from the captors, her shrill cry
Stealing in fitful echoes from afar,
Deepen'd the mother's death-pang.

Eve drew on,
And from his toil the husband and the sire
Turn'd wearied home. With wondering thought he mark'd
No little feet came forth to welcome him;
No Lily of the Vale, who first of all
Was wont to espy him.

Through the house he rush'd
Empty and desolate, and down the wild.
There lay his wife, all weltering in her blood,
Upon the trampled grass. In vain he bore
The form of marble to its couch, and strove
Once more to vivify that spark of life
Which ruthless rage had quench'd.

On that dread hour

Of utter desolation, broke a cry,
"Oh, father! father!" and around his neck
Two weeping children wound their trembling arms,
Saved mid the thicket's tangled depths, to share
The burden of his wo.
With tireless zeal,
That sad dismember'd household sought the child
Reft from their arms, and oft with shuddering thought
Revolved the horrors that must mark her lot,
If life were hers. And when the father lay
In his last, mortal sickness, he enjoin'd
His children never to remit their search
For the lost Lily.
Years roll'd on their course;
The boy became a man, and o'er his brow
Stole the white, sprinkled hairs. Around his hearth
Were children's children, and one pensive friend,
His melancholy sister, night and day
Mourning the lost. At length, a rumour came
Of a white woman found in Indian tents,
Far, far away. A father's dying words
Came o'er the husbandman, and up he rose,
And took his sad-eyed sister by the hand,
Blessing his household, as he bade farewell,
For their uncertain pilgrimage.
They prest

O'er cloud-capp'd mounts, through forests dense with shade,
O'er bridgeless rivers, swoln to torrents hoarse,
O'er prairies like the never-ending sea,
Following the chart that had been dimly traced
By stranger-guide.
At length they reach'd a lodge
Deep in the wilderness, beside whose door
A wrinkled woman with the Saxon brow
Sate coarsely mantled in her blanket-robe,
The Indian pipe between her shrivell'd lips.
Yet in her blue eye dwelt a gleam of thought,
A hidden memory, whose electric force
Thrill'd to the fount of being, and reveal'd
The kindred drops that had so long wrought out
A separate channel.
With affection's haste
The sister clasp'd her neck. "Oh lost and found!
Lily! dear sister! praise to God above!"
Then in wild sobs her trembling voice was lost.
The brother drew her to his side, and bent
A long and tender gaze into the depths
Of her clear eye. That glance unseal'd the scroll
Of many years. Yet no responding tear
Moisten'd her cheek, nor did she stretch her arms
To answer their embrace.
"Oh, Lily! love!

For whom this heart so many years hath kept
Its dearest place," the sister's voice resumed,
"Hast thou forgot the home, the grassy bank
Where we have play'd? The blessed mother's voice
Bidding us love each other? and the prayer
With which our father at the evening hour
Commended us to God?"

Slowly she spake:
"I do remember, dimly, as a dream,
A brook, a garden, and two children fair,
A loving mother with a bird-like voice,
Teaching us goodness; then a trace of blood,
A groan of death, a lonely captive's pain;
But all are past away.

Here is my home,
These are my daughters.

If ye ask for him,
The eagle-eyed and lion-hearted chief,
My fearless husband, who the battle led,
There is his grave."

"Go back, and dwell with us,
Back to thy people, to thy father's God,"
The brother said. "I have a happy home,
A loving wife and children. Thou shalt be
Welcome to all. And these, thy daughters too,
The dark-eyed and the raven-hair'd, shall be

Unto me as mine own. My heart doth yearn
O'er thee, our hapless mother's dearest one.
Let my sweet home be thine."

A trembling nerve
Thrill'd all unwonted at her bosom's core,
And her lip blanch'd. But the two daughters gazed
Reproachfully upon her, to their cheek
Rushing the proud Miami chieftain's blood,
In haughty silence. So, she wept no tears;
The moveless spirit of the race she loved
Had come upon her, and her features show'd
Slight touch of sympathy.

"Upon my head
Rest sixty winters. Scarcely seven were past
Among the pale-faced people. Hate they not
The red man in their heart? Smooth Christian words
They speak, but from their touch we fade away
As from the poisonous snake.

Have I not said
Here is my home? and yonder is the bed
Of the Miami chief? Two sons who bore
His brow, rest on his pillow.

Shall I turn
My back upon my dead, and bear the curse
Of the great Spirit?"

Through their feathery plumes,

Her dark-eyed daughters mute approval gave
To these stern words.
Yet still, with faithful zeal,
The brother and the sister waited long
In patient hope. If on her brow they traced
Aught like relenting, fondly they implored,
"Oh Lily! go with us!" and every tale
That pour'd o'er childhood's days a flood of light
Had the same whisper'd burden.
Oft they walk'd
Beside her, when the twilight's tender hour,
Or the young moonlight, blendeth kindred hearts
So perfectly together. But in vain;
For with the stony eye of prejudice,
Which gathereth coldness from an angel's smile.
She look'd upon their love.
And so they left
Their pagan sister in her Indian home,
And to their native vale of Wyoming
Turn'd mournful back. There, often steep'd in tears,
At morn or evening, rose the earnest prayer,
That God would keep in their lost Lily's soul
The seed her mother sow'd, and by His grace
So water it that they might meet in heaven.

TWILIGHT.

THERE is a dimness, like a doubt,
That wrappeth earth and sky,
When Day hath in its glory died,
And ere the Night comes forth with pride
Of sable majesty.

'Tis like the soft delay of Youth,
Where Love hath built its throne;
A coy reluctance, ere it rest
Entirely on another's breast,
To be no more its own.

It is the gentle pause of Heaven,
E'en as a mother mild,
Before some new bequest is lent,
Inquireth how the last was spent
Of her forgetful child.

Then Conscience, like that fearful cry
Mid Eden's deep repose,

"Where is thy brother?" turns its ray
Upon the annal of the Day,
That to its funeral goes.

Perchance, the queenly Moon descends,
And lo! the haughty Sea
On her pale face doth fix his eye,
And bids his mightiest tides comply,
And own her regency.

Yet Twilight gray to me is dear,
More than the blushing Day,
Or noontide's plenitude of light,
Or sober certainty of Night,
Or Moon with silver ray.

For then, at scepter'd Memory's call,
Long buried years awake,
And tread in charméd circles back,
With music, o'er their flowery track,
Their ancient seats to take.

And parted friends, of whom we say,
In beds of clay they rest,
Bend meekly down from glory's sphere,
And with their angel smile, or tear
Allure us to the blest.

THE UNRIFLED CABINET.

"Then shall we no more look into our cabinet, and miss its treasures."—

BAXTER.

WHEN shall that time be? When?
So many buds
We shelter'd in the garden of our heart,
Yet ere their young sheaths open'd to the sun,
They curl'd their leaves and died, we shrink to fill
Their vacant places, lest the same sharp grief
And trouble come upon us. Life doth seem,
With all its banners of felicity,
Like the fair alcove of the bard, and seat
Illusory, on which we find no rest.*

In the mind's store-house, gold we had, and gems
Gather'd from many a tome. The key we gave
To Memory, and she hath betray'd her trust.

---

* The author of the Night Thoughts had in his garden an alcove, with the representation of a seat so well painted as to deceive most observers. Near it was the inscription,

"Invisibilia non decipiunt."

The things unseen do not deceive us.

For when we ask of her, she saith that years
And sleepless cares disturb'd her, till she lost
Our stewardship of thought. When shall it be
That we may hoard for intellect, nor find
The work-day World, or stealthy Time, a thief?

Leases of tenements amid the sands
And on the cloud, papers and bonds we had,
In Earth's handwriting, well endorsed and seal'd
By smooth-tongued Hope.
They're lost! The lock is forced!
The casket rifled! All our treasures gone!
And only a brown cobweb in their place,
Spun by some mocking spider.
Still, ye say
We may obtain a cabinet, whose hoard
Robber, nor faithless friend, nor rust of years,
Shall e'er invade.
When shall that time be? When?

When Heaven's pure gate unfoldeth, and thy soul
Glides like a sunbeam through.
Then shall it be.

TALK WITH TIME AT THE CLOSE OF THE YEAR.

TIME, old Time, with the forelock gray,
While the year in its dotage doth pass away,
Come, sit by my hearth, ere the embers fail,
And hang the scythe on yon empty nail,
And tell me a tale 'neath this wintry sky
Of the deeds thou hast done as its months swept by.

"I have cradled the babe in the churchyard wide;
From the husband's arms I have taken the bride;
I have cloven a path through the Ocean's floor,
Where many have sunk to return no more;
I have humbled the strong with their dauntless breast,
And laid the old with his staff to rest.

"I have loosen'd the stone on the ruin's height,
Where the curtaining ivy grew rank and bright;
I have startled the maid in her couch of down,
With a sprinkle of white mid her tresses brown;
I have rent from his idols the proud man's hold,
And scatter'd the hoard of the miser's gold."

"Is this all? Are thy chronicles traced alone
On the riven heart and the burial-stone?"
"No, Love's young chain I have twined with flowers,
Have awaken'd a song in the rose-crown'd bowers;
Proud trophies have rear'd to the sons of fame
And paved the road for the cars of flame..

"Look to yon child, it hath learn'd of me
The word that it lisps at the mother's knee;
Look to the sage, who from me hath caught
Intenser fire for his heavenward thought;
Look to the saint, who hath nearer trod
Toward the angel hosts near the Throne of God.

"I have planted seeds in the soul, that bear
The fruits of heaven in a world of care;
I have breathed on the tear till its orb grew bright
As the diamond drop in the realms of light:
Question thy heart, hath it e'er confest
A germ so pure, or a tear so blest?"

But the clock struck twelve from the steeple gray,
And he seized his hour-glass, and strode away;
Yet his hand at parting I fear'd to clasp,
For I saw the scythe in its earnest grasp,
And read in the glance of his upward eye
His secret league with Eternity.

MAN'S THREE GUESTS.

A KNOCKING at the castle-gate
When the bloom was on the tree,
And the youthful master, all elate,
Himself came forth to see.
A jocund lady waited there,
Gay was her robe, of colours rare,
Her tresses bright to the zephyr stream'd,
And her car on its silver axle gleam'd,
Like the gorgeous barge of that queen of yore,
Whose silken sail and flashing oar
Sparkling Cydnus proudly bore.
The youth, enraptured at her smile,
And won by her enchanting wile
And flatteries vain,
Welcomed her in, with all her train,
Placing her in the chiefest seat,
While as a vassal at her feet
He knelt, and paid her homage sweet.

She deck'd his halls with garlands gay,
Bidding the sprightly viol play,
Till by her magic power
Day turn'd to night, and night to day,
For every fleeting hour
Bow'd to Pleasure as its queen;
And so, that siren guest, of mirthful mien,
Linger'd till the vernal ray
And summer's latest rose had sigh'd itself away.

A knocking at the gate!
And the lordling of the hall,
A strong and bearded man withal,
Held parley at the threshold-stone
In the pomp of his estate.
And then the warder's horn was blown,
The ponderous bolts drawn one by one,
And slowly in, with sandals torn,
Came a pilgrim, travel-worn.
A burden at his back he bare,
And coldly said, "My name is Care!"
Plodding and weary years he brought,
And a pillow worn with ceaseless thought;
And bade his votary ask of Fame,
Or Wealth, or wild Ambition's claim,
Payment for the toil he taught.

But dark with dregs was the cup he quaff'd,
And mid his harvest proud
The mocking tare looked up and laugh'd
Till his haughty heart was bow'd,
And wrinkles on his forehead hung, and o'er his path a cloud.

Again, a knocking at the gate
At the wintry eventide,
And querulous was the voice that cried,
"Who cometh here so late?"
"Ho! rouse the sentinel from his sleep,
Strict guard at every loop-hole keep!"
And "man the towers!" he would have said,
But alas! his early friends were dead,
And his eagle glance was awed,
And a frost that never thaw'd
Had settled on his head.
But that thundering at the gate
From morn till midnight late,
Knew no rest,
And a boding tone of fate,
Like an owlet's cry of hate,
Chill'd his breast.
Yet he raised the palsied hand,
And, eager, gave command
To repel the threatening guest.

So the Esculapian band,
In their armour old and tried,
Were summon'd to his side,
And the watchful nurses came,
Whose lamp, like vestal flame,
Never died.
But the tottering bulwarks their trust betray'd,
And the old man groan'd as a breach was made;
Then through the chasm a skeleton foot
Forced its way,
And a fleshless hand to a shaft was put,
And he was clay.

THE END.